one 02 /BRA

Writing You

Writing Your Doctoral Dissertation
Invisible Rules for Success

Rita S. Brause

RoutledgeFalmer
Taylor & Francis Group
LONDON AND NEW YORK

First published 2000
by RoutledgeFalmer
11 New Fetter Lane, London EC4P 4EE

Simultaneously published in the USA and Canada
by RoutledgeFalmer
Garland Inc., 19 Union Square West, New York, NY 10003

Reprinted 2003, 2004 by RoutledgeFalmer

RoutledgeFalmer is an imprint of the Taylor & Francis Group

Typeset in Times by Taylor & Francis Books Ltd
Printed and bound in Great Britain by
Biddles Ltd., King's Lynn, Norfolk

British Library Cataloguing in Publication Data
A catalogue record for this book is available from the British Library

Library of Congress Cataloging in Publication Data
Brause, Rita S.
  Writing your doctoral dissertation: invisible rules for success / Rita S.
  Brause.
    p. cm.
Includes bibliographical references and index.
  1. Dissertation, Academic Handbooks, manuals, etc. 2. Report writing
  Handbooks, manuals, etc. I. Title.
    LB2369.B72 2000
  808.02–dc21   99–39560

ISBN 0–750–70744–5

This book is dedicated to those who seek to succeed and those who support their success:

- doctoral students who are committed to completing their dissertations;
- doctoral faculty who are dedicated to promoting student success while subtly revising the process;

And

- my family – starting with my parents – Jack and Ruth Brause – and continuing with my sister and brothers – Roberta, Louis, and Barry – each personally successful, while constantly helping others achieve their goals.

Contents

Contents

Figures and Tables

Figures

Tables

Preface

For the past twenty-five years I have been working with doctoral students, guiding their evolution to doctoral recipients. During the time we work together, I become intensely conscious of their need to understand the culture of the university as it impacts on their progress. Concurrently, they need to be receptive to engaging in a transformative, life-changing experience, the essence of learning. As I recall my own days as a doctoral student, I remember being at a total loss to understand what was happening to me. I have discovered this is not unique. Most have no idea what a dissertation looks like or how it evolves.

While most doctoral students expect to draw on their earlier collegiate experiences, nothing in the academic world prepares them for the complexity and intensity inherent in the doctoral process. I have identified the crucial issues to include in *Writing Your Dissertation: Invisible Rules for Success* from multiple sources:

- my experience in guiding more than seventy-five doctoral dissertations to completion;
- more than 200 anonymous responses by doctoral students and graduates to open-ended questionnaires;
- focus groups with doctoral students and graduates; and
- informal conversations with current doctoral students and graduates, including some of whom teach in doctoral programs across the nation.

Increasing numbers of adults are receiving doctoral degrees (Magner, 1999), but it is a culture in which most admit a lack of knowledge of the rules. They frequently search for explicit information about what this complex, highly interactive, academic, social, and political process involves. Access to knowledgeable sources of information is limited, yet essential for emotional and intellectual survival. This book serves as a practical guide for students to progress in planning, writing, and defending their dissertations.

When students seek to understand the rules of the program, they are frequently referred to the university *Bulletin* or told to see their advisor. There is little explicit documentation of what occurs in a doctoral program. What is particularly missing from these sources is information about the human element, the social interactions which are the hallmark of doctoral programs, and probably the most problematic for most doctoral students. Recognizing the need to address this gap, I have developed a comprehensive guide to many dimensions of the doctoral process, particularly focusing on the writing of the doctoral dissertation.

While the primary goal in writing this book is to help current doctoral students to survive and flourish in their programs, I have also become aware of the need to consider major reforms in the doctoral process. This has been supported by recent publications (e.g.: Kennedy, 1997; Lovitts, 1996; Menand, 1996; Olson and Drew, 1998). For current enrollees, survival is probably the key issue, but from a long-term perspective, I think we in the academic world need to reflect on what is expected of students, and find ways to create more supportive settings for students and the academic community-at-large. While the primary audience for *Writing your Doctoral Dissertation* is current students, doctoral students may find it productive to share this book with friends and relatives, helping them to understand and provide more supportive settings in completing a dissertation. In addition, graduates have impressed me with their desire, now that they are done, to compare their experiences with others, as well as to obtain a clearer sense of the totality of the experience. Certainly faculty would benefit from understanding the students' perspectives as well.

Each academic institution creates unique rules and procedures for completing a doctoral degree, but there are many similarities across institutions. *Writing your Doctoral Dissertation* offers a combination of the general rules, along with strategies for coping with the range of experiences you may encounter in your progress. The book will prepare you for some of the likely hurdles, offering guidance to avoiding conflicts, and to working through problems which are impossible to predict but will inevitably occur. I frequently remind you to "check with your advisor," "check with your peer-support group," "check with your chair." These individuals know your local terrain. The more information you have, the more prepared you will be to address each of the issues in your program and to handle your unique experiences.

A case could be made that doctoral students are required to be the most rigorous researchers. Researchers are resourceful, seeking information in a wide array of sites. As a reader of this book, you are a researcher. *Writing your Doctoral Dissertation* supplements any materials available at your institution. It cannot supplant any institutional documents or explanatory requirements. Read all publications from your institution which enumerate the steps in the process, as well as any academic calendars which might offer clues about mandated activities (e.g. preliminary examinations, matriculation interviews, oral defenses) and their frequency of occurrence (e.g. once each semester, annually). The *Bulletin* is a good starting point, but don't stop there. Look for brochures, pamphlets, fliers, bulletin board notices, advertisements in campus newspapers, and program newsletters. Explore the materials available in the Graduate Office and the Office of the Dean of Graduate Studies, or like, which might describe some of the requirements. Inquire about program meetings, informal gatherings, and advisement materials which may offer a map of what to expect.

To obtain the information contained in these pages, I have engaged in intensive research, obtaining numerous lenses on this phenomenon which we call "going for my doctorate." Some 250 people provided information on their own experiences as doctoral students and doctoral advisors. Within the text, and as epigraphs at the beginning of chapters, you will see direct quotations from these sources. For more information about my research procedures, see Brause (1997) and Appendix A. A critique of the doctoral process based on this research is in preparation.

While there are increasing numbers of books which are outlining the parts of a dissertation (see Appendix B for some useful titles), there is a need for students to understand both the academic and the social elements which contribute to their progress. This book combines both of these elements as it provides step-by-step guidance in moving from identifying a research problem to defending your dissertation. Most students in doctoral programs proceed through the steps with only a vague understanding of what a dissertation is or what is involved in getting one. Having a sense of typical issues, you will be ready for what lies ahead for you.

This book will probably be useful to read in two ways:

- first, as a quick read – offering an *overview* of "the terrain" and an explanation of all the steps in the process of writing a dissertation;
- second, as ready reference – providing a *step-by-step guide* to creating your committee, writing your proposal, and preparing for your oral defense, for example.

I expect that you will initially review the total contents, noting the range of information, realizing the impossibility of attending to all the details, but happy to know that they are available for later reference. Recognizing the depth of detail provided, you will intelligently read carefully up to the point where you are in writing your dissertation. Then, you will read the next chapter v-e-r-y s-l-o-w-l-y. You will refer to each chapter in turn, as you progress through your research apprenticeship. (This assumption follows from Gail Sheehy (1976)'s experience with *Passages: Predictable Crises of Adult Life*, in which people tended to read to the chapter which represented their current stage, and deferred reading subsequent chapters until the time when they were at that next stage.) Each person will start this intense reading at a different place, eventually proceeding to the final chapters as you triumph in writing your doctoral dissertation. I am writing this book as a student advocate. I acknowledge there are numerous, significant problems in the process, many of which were highlighted in the process of collecting the data for this book. The most notable event was the recent suicide of a doctoral student which was attributed to university procedures that isolated students and made them vulnerable to the whims of one faculty member (see Schneider, 1998). For students to make an informed commitment to a doctoral program, there is a need to know what's expected: to prepare themselves and their significant others for the time and emotional pressures likely to develop; to participate more knowledgeably in the process; and to take advantage of the wealth of opportunities available in this process.

Writing Your Dissertation makes explicit the invisible culture of dissertation writing and thereby increases the likelihood of your success, avoiding the possibility that you will drop out of your program never having a clue about what was really expected. You will never be the same person you were before your doctoral experience. I hope that by reading this book you will find yourself much enriched by the process of completing your doctoral program.

There are three major parts to this book which correspond to the several stages involved in writing a dissertation. Initially you will need an overview, offered in Part I, entitled "Getting a sense of the terrain." Part II is called "Preparing for your study," and Part III provides details for "Doing your study." The appendixes contain resources, specifically a sample checklist for documenting your progress; suggestions for reading on the dissertation, the academic world, and research methodology; and a presentation of some of my research findings from the study of the dissertation process.

Your experiences as a doctoral student will be memorable. I hope you will have many happy memories. I encourage your comments and questions about each section along with suggestions for improving this volume for future doctoral students.

Acknowledgments

Writing this book has taken a tremendous amount of cooperation from friends near and far, and many anonymous participants. The written responses which arrived daily in the mail postmarked from most of the fifty states and a few from other nations provided a depth of information about dissertations that is unprecedented. The lengthy and emotionally charged statements confirmed the need for this book as well as the need for rethinking the dissertation process.

I am indebted to the 250 anonymous respondents to the questionnaire and to the individuals who participated in roundtable discussions and individual interviews about their experiences in their dissertation programs. These included: Maria Cataneo, Sr. St. John Delaney, Jane Dorian, Rita Guare, Louis Guinta, John Houtz, Rita King, Stephen Kucer, Sandra Lanzone, Della Levine, Lewis Levine, Kathy Malu, Lillian Masters, Brian Monahan, William Ronzitti, Rita Seidenberg, Michael Shaw, Robert J. Starratt, Clifford Williams, and Jean Winter. Their comments about the need for this book helped me to keep going when times were tough. At conferences when I talked about this project, I also received support for this project from doctoral students at numerous, anonymous institutions. The office of Research at Fordham University also provided important support.

I would like to acknowledge, with thanks, permission to reproduce the drawings on pages 13 and 29 to Kelly A. Clark and Scott Arthur Maesar respectively.

This book has benefited greatly from the careful reading of early drafts by Kathy Malu, Renée Frank Holtz, Jackie Stone, and Cliff Williams. They each provided different lenses through which to view the book. Kathy, particularly, read and read and read again – never being worn down by the numerous drafts which this text has gone through.

Malcolm Clarkson had faith early on that I could do this. His vote of confidence helped me to bring this to completion as well. As the manuscript progressed, I benefited from enthusiastic responses from Anna Clarkson and Shankari Sanmuganathan.

Most of all, I am indebted to my family and friends who nudged me when I needed it, and celebrated with me when I was done. These included Roberta Brause, Christine Donohue, Jane Dorian, Lou Guinta, Dorothy Kirshenberg, Stephen Kucer, Sandra Lanzone, Kathy Malu, Brian Monahan, Alice Ryan, Rita Seidenberg, and Michael Shaw.

Acknowledgments

I am so happy the day has come when I feel like I have done the best I can – and await your comments and suggestions. I wish you luck and strength!

January 1999

Part I
Getting a Sense of the Terrain

1 Comparing a Dissertation to a Long Term Paper

I affirmed that I can achieve a goal I set for myself by using intelligence, a combination of prior experience, hard work, determination, and focused effort.

Writing a dissertation is not a difficult task once you have established your priorities and have the desire to complete it. I had the desire and made writing the dissertation a priority in my life. My will and determination helped me along the way.

Nothing you have done in your academic career is quite like writing a dissertation. But there are resemblances – to term papers, for example. Drawing on your wealth of experiences with term papers will expedite your dissertation writing. You have considerable familiarity with writing term papers. With those proficiencies in place, it is now useful to bring them to a level of consciousness.

Writing a term paper entails not only writing *per se*, but necessitates extensive reading and learning – prior to and during the writing process. The same holds true for your dissertation writing. Your learning and understanding of the topic you are studying will be magnified many times in the process of writing your dissertation. Writing a paper promotes learning, as does writing a dissertation. In the process of writing your dissertation you will learn many things:

- You will learn more about your discipline.
- You will learn more about writing to an audience beyond the one professor who taught the course, extending to your dissertation committee and ultimately your academic discipline globally.
- You will learn to organize large chunks of information.
- You will learn to do original research.
- You will learn to organize your time so that you are as productive as you want to be.

Most dissertation writers find this experience amazing *in retrospect*. Writing a dissertation is a true learning experience writ large. A contrast between the term papers you've written and the dissertation is useful.

Clearly you have been successful in your paper writing. The successes you have accumulated over the span of your academic career on smaller projects provide the confidence that you can meet this new challenge of writing your dissertation.

You know that a dissertation is a lengthy document which is written by a graduate student in the process of completing a doctoral degree. You also know that writing a dissertation includes: reporting on research, working with a committee and a chair, and having "orals." But beyond these vague labels, there is generally little understanding of this virtually invisible activity within universities. Chances are that one of your strengths as a student has been your ability to write acceptable, even highly praised, term papers. You appropriately expect to draw on that experience in your dissertation writing.

You might assume that the coursework preceding your dissertation prepares you for writing your dissertation, particularly thinking of all the term paper writing required in your courses. Clearly those experiences will be useful, but it's important to understand that writing a dissertation is both different from and similar to a term paper.

Writing a Dissertation

If we look at just the title page of a dissertation, we will have access to additional information about dissertations. The title page gives us useful insights into the total document if we examine it very closely. As you study Figure 1.1, consider the information which you can infer from this one page and jot these down.

Now that you've had a chance to think about some inferences, we can identify some of the information explicitly and implicitly provided on the title page of Rebecca Strear's dissertation:

- The spacing of information on the page suggests the dissertation is a formal document with a prescribed format, distinct from most other writing we have seen.
- The use of technical terms in the title (e.g. "Professional Development Schools") suggests the text is addressed to a small subset of our society which is familiar with the technical language.
- The title of the dissertation is highly focused. From the title we can identify unique characteristics:

  - There is an analysis of data. (A special type of analysis will be reported; a qualitative analysis will be reported.)
  - The source for the data which informs the study is identified. (The perceptions of teachers will be studied.)
  - The research reports on a highly focused issue. (Only the issue of teacher *perceptions* of collaboration will be investigated, excluding, for example, any documentation of their collaborations.)

Figure 1.1   *Title page from dissertation: sample A*

A QUALITATIVE ANALYSIS OF
TEACHERS' PERCEPTIONS OF COLLABORATION
WITHIN PROFESSIONAL DEVELOPMENT SCHOOLS

REBECCA S. STREAR

BA, City College of New York, 1983
MS, Teachers College, Columbia University, 1989

Committee
Renée S. Browne, EdD, Chair
Andrew N. Baranyai, EdD
Richard S. Hayes, PhD

DISSERTATION
SUBMITTED IN PARTIAL FULFILLMENT OF THE REQUIREMENTS
FOR THE DEGREE OF DOCTOR OF PHILOSOPHY
IN THE GRADUATE SCHOOL OF EDUCATION OF
XXXXXXXXXX UNIVERSITY

1997

- The data are collected in a restricted setting. (The site for these collaborations is restricted to places identified as "Professional Development
  Schools.")

- The academic history of the degree candidate is documented.
- The dissertation is the product of collaboration among "the Committee,"
  along with Strear.
- Each member of the committee holds a doctoral degree.
- One of these individuals on the committee is identified as "Chair."
- The dissertation is not the only requirement for the doctoral degree; there
  are additional requirements.
- A word processor or computer is used in the writing or at least in the
  presentation of the dissertation.

Just from studying the title page, one slice of data, we have identified important
elements of a dissertation. But this is only one source. We need to compare this

with other data before we make any hasty generalizations or assumptions. And so, let's look at another title page from a dissertation completed at a different university, as presented in Figure 1.2.

We can compare Figures 1.1 and 1.2. They both have lengthy, descriptive titles, names of committee members, and a statement about the "partial fulfillment of requirements" for a degree. They both have a formal, professional presentation style. On some level they look fairly similar, with relatively minor variations. Jot down any additional information you can infer about dissertations from these two samples before reading my interpretation.

Combining our insights from samples A and B, we know that:

- these are title pages from dissertations, not dissertation proposals or term papers;
- dissertations may use different research methodologies; and

Figure 1.2 *Title page from dissertation: sample B*

Dissertation Committee:
Professor Tom Jones, Chairman,
Professor Eric R. Green, and
Professor Harriet Stern

A COMPARISON OF THE WRITING ACTIVITIES

OF FIFTH GRADE STUDENTS

IN AN URBAN ELEMENTARY SCHOOL

AND AN URBAN MIDDLE SCHOOL

Michael Schlesinger

Submitted in partial fulfillment of the

requirements for the degree of Doctor of

Philosophy in the School of Education of

XXXXXXXX University

1997

- the style of the presentation suggests a required format rather than a unique one created by each individual student.

There are also several contrasts, some of which might indicate subtle differences in the relationship between the student and the committee. These nuances may have little import for you, or they may suggest a specific stance which you should consider adopting in your conversations with your committee, for example.

- The role of the committee is not clear. In sample A the committee members are listed below the student's name, implying that they *supported* the student's work, whereas in sample B the positioning of the committee on the top of the page may suggest that the committee *directed* the dissertation.
- The prominence of the student's name differs: in sample A the doctoral student's name is all in upper case letters, equivalent to the emphasis given to the title of the dissertation. In sample B the name appears in upper and lower case letters, similar to the listing for the committee.
- In one institution, the doctoral degrees (EdD or PhD) held by the committee members are noted, whereas the other institution seems to emphasize the fact that the committee is comprised of professors.
- Only in sample A is there a notation of the degrees previously awarded to the doctoral candidate.

These sample title pages offer us an initial sense of the many issues involved in writing a dissertation.

Writing a Term Paper

In writing your term papers, you followed what your professor directed you to do, in the main. Your professors monitored your pace. Many, if not all, of the sources which you referred to in your paper were suggested by your professor. The topic of your paper was probably predetermined by your professor and you had a deadline to meet. Your term paper usually comprised one element in a total evaluation of your work in the course, eventually resulting in the professor entering a grade with the registrar which indicated that you had successfully completed the course. Whether you received a grade of B or A may have been the most important outcome for you. For most, the completion of that requirement yielded great relief and satisfaction. Few concerned themselves with making sense of the course in the context of their other studies.

At this time we have sufficient information to document our growing understanding of some of the differences and similarities between term papers and dissertations. In addition to the insights we have developed from these brief analyses, there are several other related issues which become noteworthy in our comparison.

- When writing a dissertation, you are expected to "break some new ground." You are expected to contribute to the evolving knowledge base of a discipline through your dissertation. In a term paper you may explore some areas in depth; there is little need to determine if others have gone this route before. In fact, everyone in your class may be writing on the same topic. In writing your dissertation, you conduct an intensive data search, insuring that the project you are mounting is different from what has "already been done." You will bring a new perspective. You will study with new lenses, becoming aware of different phenomena. Your study will contribute to the expanding literature in your field.

- When you write a term paper, you are aware of a professor's biases and you probably deal with these in the writing of your paper. When writing your dissertation you have many more readers of your work – potentially readers with different, conflicting theoretical orientations. It will be essential for you to deal with this potential conflict, discussing competing theories and ideas. Ultimately, your interpretation of your data will need to reflect an understanding of multiple viewpoints.

- In contrast to your term papers, which probably drew on sources recommended by your professor, your dissertation will reflect your resourcefulness at identifying pertinent sources. In fact, in the process of writing your dissertation, you become the expert, in contrast to your term papers where your professor typically was more knowledgeable than you on the topic.

- A term paper is returned to the student, with no record of that paper remaining at the institution. Certainly it is not freely available to those within and outside the university. Your dissertation, however, will be available to the entire academic community through *Dissertation Abstracts International* and through Interlibrary loan, for example.

- It is very important to acknowledge that your relationships with the members of your dissertation committee will influence the progress you make. While a course has a fixed conclusion date, your dissertation does not.

- When writing term papers, you wrote independently. Writing your dissertation *requires* collaboration with your committee.

- A term paper is a one-shot deal, usually. You turn in the paper, it is read and evaluated, and sometimes returned with a grade and/or comments. With a dissertation, typically there are numerous drafts. No longer is it acceptable to get a passing grade or helpful comments. Now you need to respond to those comments. These remarks and questions become directions for improving your text, as well as guidelines for future drafts and future parts of your dissertation. Your dissertation is a work in progress. Your committee's input seeks to promote the possibility of attaining some level of perfection.

- In contrast to a term paper, which usually must be completed within the time-frame of a one-semester course, your dissertation has no such time limits. One of the distinguishing characteristics of a dissertation is that it goes through multiple drafts before it finally receives the approval of the committee. In fact, frequently there is a "dissertation proposal," which needs to be approved prior to the initiation of the dissertation research project. This proposal then serves as a start for the dissertation, which is revised to document the actual study.

- A dissertation is frequently developed chapter by chapter, or chapter part by chapter part, with the student gradually working towards completing the total document while receiving comments along the way. Term papers are usually submitted for evaluation in their entirety.

- While writing a term paper is a fairly private experience, with the professors typically being the sole readers of your paper, your dissertation becomes a public document. Others may engage you in conversation about your study. Those on your committee will talk with you about your work. Your program peers will talk with you about your progress and your findings. And you will identify conferences and journals sponsored by your professional organizations as settings where your ideas may be shared as well.

- Friends and associates outside of your program will ask about your progress in completing your dissertation. With little understanding of what it means to write a dissertation, their inquiries, while well-intentioned, may create unwanted pressure. The number of times they inquire about your dissertation will exceed the number of times when they asked about a term paper.

- When friends hear that you are working on a dissertation, they may engage you in an extended conversation about your topic, an unusual occurrence when you are writing a term paper. They may offer their own insights, which, although unsolicited, may become useful in the process of completing your dissertation.

Table 1.1 identifies some important issues in comparing these two experiences.

In many respects, your successes in writing term papers were brief forays, preparation for the extended journey of writing your dissertation. To provide you with additional confidence, I strongly urge you to go to your university library and find the section where the dissertations are located. Choose one written by someone you know, or by a potential dissertation chair, or at random, and study it. While at this time you are a tourist, ultimately it will become your "native land." The best way to change from being a tourist to becoming a native is to put down roots and stay for a while, becoming familiar and comfortable with the customs. Your first 30-minute trip will whet your desire to learn more and you will return many times to this section of the library for advice and confirmation.

Table 1.1   *A comparison of term papers and dissertations*

Term papers	Dissertations
one professor assigns topics	collaboration with several professors
fulfills one requirement for one course	fulfills one requirement for a degree
fixed completion date	no fixed completion date
fairly private matter	available to public
format of minor importance	format is monitored
explores one issue superficially	explores one issue in depth
documents knowledge	advances knowledge in the field
limited, familiar audience	wide, unknown audience
professor guides access to resources	work mainly independent
provides evidence of learning	provides evidence of scholarship
written independently	written in collaboration with committee
one opportunity	multiple drafts, multiple revisions
graded as A, B, C, etc.	graded Pass or Fail
restricted time period (15 weeks)	unlimited time
submitted in entirety at one time	submitted chapter by chapter
restricted in length	lengthy, comprehensive document
explicit instructions	evolving, personally created project
use notetaking, research and word-processing skills	use notetaking, research and word-processing skills
limited feedback when in-process	extensive in-process feedback
little time for personal critique	constant personal critique essential
little attention to securing materials	paranoid about securing materials

2 Jumping through Hoops, Going on a Journey

Personal Metaphors for the Process

Successfully completing the dissertation process brings enormous exhilaration!

The deeper your education, the more it will change you. (That's why it's so important to choose carefully what you study and with whom.)

(Booth et al., 1995, p. 9)

When we think about "writing a dissertation" we may envision a person seated at a computer for long hours, creating hundreds of pages of text, surrounded by stacks of books and documents. While this is an appropriate image, it clearly does not capture the totality of the experience. In fact, it represents only a small part, perhaps 10 per cent of all that goes into writing the dissertation. Many who have gone through the process comment that only those who have been there could understand what it's like. To facilitate your understanding, we will look at the metaphors which pepper the conversations of doctoral students.

Metaphors for Dissertation Writing

Dissertation writers frequently describe the process through powerful images and metaphors. They vividly convey the intensity of the experience and the strong emotions – positive and negative – involved in the process. Some consider the process to be much like a *Byzantine maze*. This suggests there are many paths, with high bushes separating them, yet no maps, clues, or knowledgeable guides to lead from entrance to exit. A candidate may go on seemingly endless treks, never confident of finding the way out.

Others talk of all the *hurdles* to be mounted or all the *hoops* to jump through. They seem to connect dissertation writing with competitive races where there are numerous fixed, human-created obstacles which the participants need to mount successfully. The hurdles are strategically placed obstacles, making the path to be traveled intentionally difficult. The hoops may change in size and location. Implicitly, too, there is one predetermined, acceptable goal and route to be followed. Malevolence is inherent in this model, suggesting that those in charge intentionally seek to make the process difficult. Those who are strong-willed, stubborn, and tenacious will prevail and succeed.

Mountain climbing, running the rapids, and *running a marathon* are also frequent analogies. While these are challenging physical exercises much like mounting hurdles, they differ in that the challenges are naturally occurring, not intentionally created. There is a sense that the individual is testing and challenging herself or himself to try more difficult activities, seeking to enhance his or her record. In these metaphors there is neither the necessity for competition with others nor a malevolent connotation. The individual who succeeds in climbing the mountain is pleased at having met a self-established challenge.

Others talk about the dissertation process as a *game.* They are focusing on the fixed end, and the identification of winners and losers in the process. In addition, there is always the possibility of playing another round with new winners. Frequently there is allusion to the fact that although this is a game, the rules either were not explained at the outset or constantly change. In this metaphor, the dissertation writer considers herself or himself to be a victim, subject to others' rules, with no power or control.

Kelly A. Clark, a doctoral student at the University of Vermont, while attending a session of the Ethnography Conference at the University of Pennsylvania in 1997, created (along with several other conference co-attenders) a Chutes and Ladders drawing to convey her sense of the complexity of the process (see Figure 2.1). They considered the dissertation process to be an uphill battle. There are numerous ladders which represent the support from faculty advisors and peers. The chutes represent the gate-keepers, and distractions from life that sidetrack their progress. For those who persevere, there is the oral defense and then a time to celebrate. Although children are known to play Chutes and Ladders for hours, the connection with the dissertation process is perhaps a cynical one, suggesting that the dissertation is one more of life's "games."

Another description of the doctoral process uses a *gardening* comparison. In this model, the doctoral candidate focuses on the slow growth process from seed to flower: the need for patient weeding, fertilizing, watering, and constant monitoring to adjust for unpredictable factors such as weather conditions and the speed of seed germination. The reaped flowers or fruit reward the intense attention to the garden. In this model, the doctoral candidate may select the seeds to plant, based, for example, on knowledge about the climate and soil conditions. Then the candidate takes responsibility for constantly monitoring their progress, and nurturing the growth of the seedlings to flowers or fruit. Additional resources may enhance the quality of the flowers or fruit, or protect them from insects or unexpected weather conditions. From this process, the gardener/dissertation writer becomes more knowledgeable and more adept at growing/writing. This metaphor suggests an optimistic stance on writing a dissertation, viewing it as an intellectual and emotional growth process with a positive, predictable outcome and little mental contribution.

Other metaphors include:

A coming of age experience A guide brings me through a brutal, mind-blowing experience, resulting in my viewing the world with new lenses, ready to face new challenges.

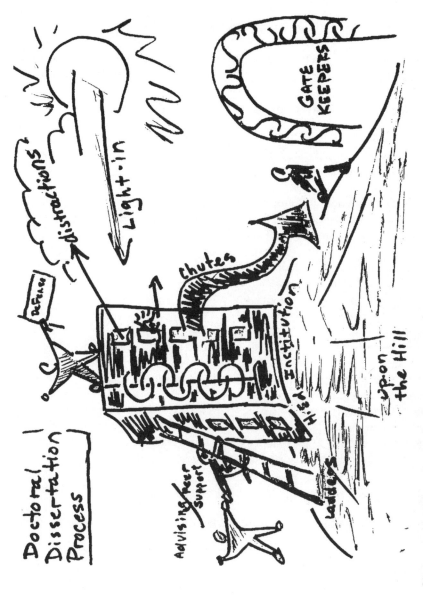

Figure 2.1   *Chutes and Ladders: the doctoral dissertation process*
Source: Kelly A. Clark

A train ride, a trip, a journey   An exploration of new terrain, having new experiences and becoming exhilarated and exhausted in the process.

An exercise, a war, a battle   An on-going conflict with no clear indication of appropriate strategies or predictable outcomes.

A hazing experience   A humiliating experience to be endured.

A birthing event   A process filled with anticipation, tension of the unknown, and ultimately, a new life along with the possibility of post-partum depression.

A blind person   An individual stumbling in a room never visited before.

A dance   An activity including finding a partner who will lead me because I'm never sure what the next step is, but know I need to depend on my partner (chair) to learn and complete the dance.

While the metaphors all conjure up different images, there are striking commonalities between them. They are all physical activities accompanied by significant affective dimensions. They are:

- memorable and emotionally complex;
- physically and intellectually challenging;
- dependent on a guide or leader; and
- processes with winners and losers.

These metaphors provide a sense of the range of experiences doctoral candidates recall. Doctoral students frequently change their metaphors as they progress. It is not uncommon to share enthusiasm with a student on a jubilant day, and to discover her or him two weeks later in a confused or frustrated state of mind. Our understanding of this general range of experiences provides an opportunity to dig deeper, to get more specific about student experience. As a way to obtain additional dimensions and a more comprehensive understanding we look in greater depth at typical doctoral students' comments.

Reflecting on the Reflections

The metaphors provide important insights in our quest to understand the doctoral process:

- Writing the dissertation involves *exposure to ideas*. For some, this is equated with learning; for others, it engenders a resistant attitude. Students develop organizational and evaluation skills; students increase the rigor of their thinking and become committed to lifelong learning; students become more adept at participating in academic dialog; students become researchers. Students learn about themselves as learners and writers in the process of writing a dissertation. Some prefer isolation, others seek collaboration.

- Doctoral students find themselves *dependent on others*. They cannot control what is happening. There is little explicit information to prepare them for the experience, explaining their frequent complaint: "No one ever told me!" There are unstated rules, and rules which change unpredictably. Without explicit information and direction, doctoral students feel vulnerable and discouraged.
- There may be *gate-keeping* going on in the process of working towards an accepted dissertation. The dissertation committee plays the role of gate-keepers. The criteria for approval of a student's dissertation are neither explicit nor predictable. One individual faculty member may delay a student's progress. Conflicts with individual faculty may return to haunt the doctoral student at a later time. Doctoral students frequently try to become mind readers, trying to figure out what the committee members want. When minds change, the student usually decides to accommodate those changes in order to expedite the process.
- The doctoral process is an intensely *emotional experience*: some people seem melancholy at some times, accepting, and even enthusiastic, at other times.
- The dissertation process is clearly a *memorable* process.
- The process of writing a dissertation is both *lengthy* and *unpredictable*.

There are clearly conflicting views represented among the student remarks. There are those who view the process as one that is not within their control, something which is virtually "being done to them." And then there are others who have a totally different experience, happily noting changes in themselves and the knowledge gained from the experience. This latter group seems to feel personally involved and takes some responsibility and credit for the changes in themselves. The former group seemingly resists any external influence, perhaps believing that the dissertation is intended to validate their existing knowledge, not expecting that there might be new, different, demanding learning experiences.

Many of these comments focus on *personal* qualities while others focus on *institutional* practices (e.g. common requirements, learning, and gate-keeping).

Personal Qualities of Doctoral Students

- tenacious, persevering, goal-directed;
- ready for numerous, unpredictable surprises; and
- flexible, collaborative, independent, and/or deferential as needed

---

Knowing that the process is both personal and bureaucratic expands our understanding of some of the dynamics involved. On the one hand, it suggests that there is not just one force controlling the process. An individual cannot write a dissertation outside of an institutional context. Dissertations are the property of institutions. Dissertations are written to fulfill institutional requirements. Individuals write dissertations in collaboration with faculty in institutions. While each committee creates a unique style of interaction, the presence of the committee structure connotes a social component of the process. Students who consider themselves independent of the institution may be deceiving themselves, not acknowledging the power of the bureaucracy. Successful doctoral students become more knowledgeable about the rules of their home institution as they navigate their dissertation waters. (This knowledge may be implicit or explicit, but it becomes evident as the candidate becomes proficient at mastering the institutional currents/rules.)

As a student in the process, you will create your own metaphor(s) for the experiences you are going through. Bringing these metaphors to a level of consciousness may promote your progress. As you consider these metaphors, it might be advantageous for you to contemplate metaphors that contribute to your progress. For example, if you flourish in circumstances where you feel victimized and totally dependent on others, then consciously choose to use the metaphors which reflect this behavior (e.g. hurdles, maze, and game). Conversely, if you pride yourself on your ability to turn any situation into one which is enjoyable and beneficial to you, then use metaphors that reflect that stance (e.g. journey and garden). Expect that these will change as you engage in the variety of activities integral to doctoral programs. The dissertation process is clearly memorable, emotionally as well as intellectually. Most students in doctoral programs proceed through the steps with only a vague understanding of what a dissertation is or what is involved in getting it done. Your reading this book is an indication of one of your strategies for taking charge of what will happen to you. An additional resource is an understanding of the academic world from the professors' viewpoint, insightfully presented in references cited in Appendix C. With this information you will be ready!

3   The Stages in Writing a Dissertation
An Overview

I was relieved and happy as I finished various stages – having my prospectus approved, passing oral exams, getting my readers to sign-off!

I didn't realize how complicated the whole process was, but I loved every minute of it!

Each community has identifiable customs: dress, food, and language. Academic communities establish rules which, when learned by those who are new to the context create a more positive experience and the potential for an extended relationship. As a doctoral student, you will want to learn the language that prevails in your doctoral program. Knowing the difference, for example, between a doctoral dissertation and a dissertation proposal, will facilitate your participation in conversations with your classmates and your professors. As you learn the technical language, you are also learning many important customs and practices.

One way to highlight these practices is to contextualize the vocabulary in an overview of the dissertation process. It is useful to know that many terms may be considered synonymous, yet each institution selects its preferred label. In one school, students may be assigned an advisor; at another an academic counselor is appointed to advise. Figure 3.1 notes many such similar terms.

There are many stages marking progress in a doctoral program, from formal admission to the official awarding of the degree. All doctoral recipients must go through all these stages. We will highlight fairly predictable stages across doctoral programs, which will help you to understand and therefore travel your local terrain more successfully.

Institutional Stages in the Process: Labels of Progress

As noted in Figure 3.2, there are four phases encompassing eight stages. Each phase is marked by a significant event: Phase I ends when you obtain provisional matriculation; Phase II is marked by the completion of coursework; Phase III ends the successful completion of the examination or candidacy experience; Phase IV ends with the approval of your dissertation.

Advancement to each stage in the process is considered an important indicator of progress from both student and faculty perspectives. While many look

Figure 3.1 *Common terms in doctoral programs*

University processes	University-related roles	Research terms
Candidacy experience	**Advisor**	**Categories for analysis**
Candidacy paper	Academic advisor	Labels
Qualifying paper	Program advisor	Possible
Comprehensive	Academic	categories
Examination	counselor	Potential categories
Preliminary	Advisor	Patterns
exams		Grouping of your data
Prelims	**Chair**	Rubrics for analysis
Generals	Dissertation chair	Variables
	Major professor	
Dissertation	Mentor	**Data**
Major study	Director	Raw data
Your research	Head of the	
The big "D"	committee	**Data analysis**
Thesis		Reduced data set
	Committee	Reducing your
Oral examination	Doctoral committee	data
Orals	Dissertation committee	Analyzing your data
Defense	Proposed committee	Analysis
Oral defense		Synthesis
Final orals	**Doctoral student**	Data reduction
Final examination	Neophyte	
Doctoral orals	researcher	**Fieldtest**
	Researcher	Feasibility study
Proposal	The reader	Pilot test
Dissertation	You	
Proposal	Apprentice	**Informant**
Prospectus	Persister	Subject
Research proposal	Student-researcher	Participant
	Student-colleagues	
Provisional matriculation	Peers	
Conditional	Classmates	
matriculation	Professional friends	
	E-mail friends	

Figure 3.2 *The academic stages in the doctoral process*

Phase I – Application/Admission Phase

Stage 1: Apply for Admission -

      Obtain Admission with Provisional Matriculation

Phase II – Coursework Phase

Stage 2: Complete Some Coursework and Seek Permanent

      Matriculation

Stage 3: Complete All Course Work

Phase III – Examination Phase

Stage 4: Pass Qualifying Examinations

Phase IV – Dissertation Phase

Stage 5: Select Dissertation Topic, Chair, and Committee

Stage 6: Draft Dissertation Proposal

Stage 7: Conduct, Analyze, and Write-up Dissertation Study

Stage 8: Prepare for Orals

---

on these stages as hurdles to overcome, others note that each stage, with its unique requirements, contributes to the growing knowledge base required to write the dissertation. And each stage marks a step closer to achieving your goal. We will rapidly review the stages which lead up to the Dissertation Phase. While there may not be an intentional "whittling down" process, this does occur. Approximately 50 per cent of those who enter doctoral programs are awarded degrees. I believe your reading this book will increase the likelihood of your success, particularly since many who drop out comment that they had no idea what to expect!

The Coursework Phase

Coursework occurs during Stages 2 and 3 of the eight-stage process. As a newly admitted student to a doctoral program, you typically enroll on a conditional or provisional basis. Your letter of admission and/or the *Bulletin* from your university will explain the "conditions" placed on your registration. A typical condition is an academic review of your record after the completion of a series of courses, perhaps 12–18 credits. After this review, you will become a permanently matriculated student.

During the time while you are provisionally matriculated, you will arrange meetings with your designated program or academic advisor who may suggest courses for study and perhaps future directions for the long haul. Advisors are usually concerned with helping students select courses which are both required to move from provisional to permanent matriculation status and which will broaden the student's knowledge in a specific academic area. Frequently you will find they teach these courses as well. You need to meet the conditions imposed on your continuation in the program. Concurrent with your status as a provisionally matriculated student, you will start your coursework.

One of your goals in taking courses is to move beyond "conditional" or "provisional" matriculation status to permanent matriculation status. In the *Bulletin* for your university you will find a description of your doctoral program along with, for example, information about the required courses and the minimum number of credits to be completed in the program. Use the information provided in the *Bulletin*, along with informal guidance from your program advisor and your student-colleagues in selecting your courses. Your advisor is likely to know the frequency with which courses will be offered and can suggest an appropriate sequence to facilitate your expanding knowledge base.

Not only will you need to enroll in the requisite courses, but you will need to adopt a useful stance as a student in these courses. Drawing on your under-graduate and graduate collegiate experiences, you are probably accustomed to completing assignments for each individual course with the goal of accumu-lating a specific number of credits for the degree. Some students approach their courses as if they were making a necklace. Each course is an isolated bead added to a long string of similarly isolated beads, which eventually form a necklace. However, if you choose courses which are connected, in particular, to your long-term goal of creating and conducting a research project based on the concepts, theories, and processes discussed in them, you will be using your learning in these courses throughout your doctoral experience.

As a doctoral student you will benefit by taking a long-term perspective on your individual courses. By considering each course as one site in an unfamiliar community, you will obtain a more cohesive perspective on your studies. By purposely creating connections between your courses, you will develop a more comprehensive understanding of the theories and practices in your discipline. Each course offers opportunities for you to prepare for your dissertation writing in specific ways. For example, you will:

- acquire more knowledge about your discipline;
- connect with related disciplines;
- explore processes for doing research in your major area;
- identify topics which seem to be at the forefront of discussion in your field;
- meet faculty with a broad range of perspectives, knowledge, and interaction styles; and
- collaborate with students in your program, speculating on potential dissertation topics.

In other words, coursework offers you a full range of experiences, all of which are *preliminary* to the writing of your dissertation. The coursework is the foundation for the project that will eventually become known as your dissertation.

One of your initial goals in taking the courses is to move from provisional to permanent matriculation status. Institutions differ in their requirements for this rite of passage. Course grades are reviewed to monitor the fact that you are meeting the minimum grade point average in the program. Feedback from your professors regarding their expectations will guide you in determining your readiness to move to this new stage.

In the main, faculty evaluate the depth of your learning as well as your effectiveness as a researcher and independent learner. Implicitly, faculty know that doctoral students need to adopt a scholarly stance as they approach the writing of their dissertation. You need to recognize this as well, and provide opportunities for the faculty to promote your development in these areas.

Some institutions conduct a written examination for several hours' duration to assess your knowledge in the areas studied early in the program. At other universities, students are required to write a brief paper. Frequently there is an interview including several faculty, some of whom might have been your instructors, one of whom might be your academic advisor, another of whom might be the program director. At this time, faculty will discuss your progress to date (referring to your papers, your examination, and your grades) as well as probe the depth of your knowledge and your commitment to completing the program.

The institution might impose additional conditions deferring for a subsequent review, any decision about permanent matriculation status. The student, learning more about the program, the faculty, and the requirements, may reconsider her or his initial decision to enroll in the program. Students who are denied permanent matriculation status may appeal the decision, seek a second hearing, or consider changing to a different program.

On passing this experience, you are admitted to permanent matriculation status. This is an important step from the faculty's perspective, since it reflects an evaluation of your academic record as well as your performance as a student in the program. From your perspective it is important for two main reasons: with permanent matriculation status you are now eligible to participate in additional, more advanced activities in the program; and you have now met formally with several faculty from the program, getting to know them better. You will proceed with the requisite coursework and other experiences, seeking now to mount the next hurdle. Once you become "permanently matriculated" you know you have passed one major hurdle in the doctoral process. Each step connotes growing confidence from the institution concerning the possibility of your completing the program.

The Examination Phase

Becoming a doctoral *candidate*, as distinct from a permanently matriculated doctoral *student*, is another mark of progress towards the degree. A doctoral student is typically admitted into candidacy on passing another hurdle. The timing of the designation of this candidacy label varies greatly across institutions. At some institutions, candidacy is acquired after completing approximately one-half of the required coursework. At others, it happens at the end of the required coursework.

Regardless of the timing of the candidacy experience, it always requires that the student demonstrate proficiency in certain areas designated by the faculty. Faculty use this activity as a way to emphasize the continuous whittling down or selection process: coursework does not automatically lead to admission to the dissertation stage.

Candidacy experiences vary. At some institutions students must achieve passing grades on examinations of several days' duration called "comprehensive examinations" or "qualifying examinations." As an alternative to these examinations, some universities require the writing of a lengthy paper addressing one key issue in the program. In writing a qualifying paper students typically synthesize information from multiple perspectives and project a series of potential research questions in need of further study. The writing of the qualifying paper immerses the doctoral student in an area of research which will frequently become the focus of the dissertation.

There may also be an oral component, in which the student meets with selected program faculty to talk about the paper or the examination along with potential research projects. During the oral exam, the faculty evaluate the depth and breadth of a student's knowledge. Potential outcomes include advising the student to take additional courses in one specific area, or requiring the rewriting of an examination or paper. Those students who are officially admitted into "candidacy" describe themselves as doctoral candidates.

Those who are at this stage are sometimes labeled as "ABD" where the letters stand for *A*ll *B*ut the *D*issertation. In many cases, this is a pejorative label referring to people who will never complete their dissertation. Candidacy is an important gatepost on the way to the dissertation itself. Doctoral students frequently celebrate this accomplishment with their peers, knowing both the success it represents and the challenges it represents.

The Dissertation Phase

Once your candidacy is established, you typically enter the Dissertation Phase. Even though in some real sense, you are "writing your dissertation" from the day you start the program, it is at the candidacy stage that this process officially starts. View your dissertation as a project through which you will explore new areas. Many doctoral students approach the dissertation believing it is a place to document their learning from their courses. This is misguided. A dissertation is the product of a personal, scholarly exploration, *building* on and extending the learning in the courses.

For many students the change in pace between the coursework and the dissertation is so dramatic that it takes a considerable amount of time to understand the new expectations. Instead of writing term papers and attending scheduled lectures and seminars, students are now, in the main, in charge of their own progress. In fact, it usually becomes the student's responsibility to create the schedule from this time forward. While there are posted deadlines for filing dissertation proposals, for example, this deadline occurs each semester and only marks a bureaucratic process. There is no institutionally scheduled date for the completion of *your* degree. There is no deadline for the writing of the dissertation proposal, or the dissertation itself, beyond time limits for completing your degree. In some real sense, the dissertation is done after the orals, when the committee finally approves it. There are a series of essential steps or stages which stand between you and having an approved dissertation. In this process you will accomplish an array of activities including:

- identify a research topic or focus;
- establish your dissertation committee including your dissertation chair and your dissertation readers;
- write a dissertation proposal in collaboration with your dissertation committee;
- obtain approval for your proposal;
- conduct an intensive research study;
- present your research in written form as a dissertation with the assistance of your committee;
- orally "defend" your dissertation; and
- obtain an approved dissertation.

While this list may appear daunting, by reading ahead you will be guided to meet all the requirements gradually. We will consider each of these steps briefly here and note how each moves you along in your process. The chapters in Parts II and III provide extensive details concerning each of these stages.

The Dissertation Committee

Your dissertation committee is comprised of faculty from your institution. (Occasionally external members are included when there is need for different expertise and/or if, for example, the candidate has contacts with an expert in the field who happens to be affiliated with another academic institution, but this is a relatively rare occurrence.) While there are usually three-member committees, the stage at which there are three members varies among institutions. Doctoral students typically start with the selection of the faculty who will be the chair of the committee. The titles differ among institutions: chair, mentor, director, or head, for example, may be used. (We will use these terms interchangeably throughout this book.) You may refer to Figure 3.1 to note the many names for these roles.

The dissertation committee is responsible for guiding your progress in developing an approved dissertation. There are two major steps in this activity: a dissertation proposal followed by a full-blown dissertation. The committee similarly goes through at least a two-stage process. There is a small (two- or three-member) group which works on the developing project, which expands to a larger group (adding on two or more members) once there is an extended document. This second group of faculty are frequently viewed as "external" or "outside" readers, reflecting the fact that they were not part of the group that contributed to the development of the proposal. Thus, the work of the committee in advising the doctoral candidate occurs within the context of the rules and expectations of the larger institution. The committee is implicitly accountable to and monitored by additional faculty from within the university.

Establishing the Chair of Your Dissertation Committee

There is actually a fairly complex dance performed around this process of selecting the chair of your dissertation committee. Since you will be working with this faculty member for an intense and extended time period, it is important to contemplate your preferred interaction style, and your learning style. (See Chapter 6 for great detail on this process.)

Once your chosen faculty member has agreed to serve as chair, you will work with your chair to identify possible committee members who are called "readers." This selection process usually includes many considerations, not the least of which is whether each person has the expertise to contribute to the evolving research project. These members are frequently identified in the process of developing the dissertation proposal. By conferring with numerous faculty as the proposal is evolving, the student is able to discern differences in enthusiasm on the part of different faculty members for the topic, and may use this as a basis for suggesting potential members to the already identified chair. Thus, concurrently with the student writing the dissertation proposal, the committee members are selected.

The selection process is not a simple one. Doctoral students do not make this selection in isolation. The chair is usually a key person in this process. Committees are typically comprised of faculty who can offer expertise in a range of areas, all contributing knowledge to the development of your research study. Considering the potential range of expectations represented in any group of faculty, it is in the student's best interests to gather faculty who typically work well together and respect each other's views.

The Dissertation Proposal

The purpose of writing a dissertation proposal is formally to "propose" to the university faculty that they support (through faculty assignment and other resources) your engagement in a specific research project. Much like funding agencies support activities in our schools based on an explicit plan of action, sometimes called a funding proposal, a dissertation proposal represents a carefully crafted project, and reflects the expertise of the individual proposing the project. The approval of a funding proposal results in a financial award of fixed dollars. An approved dissertation proposal results in a contract between the student and the university, with specific faculty designated to support the project, each with specific roles, such as "chair" or "reader." The dissertation proposal then precedes the writing of the dissertation. (See Chapter 10 for an extended discussion of this process.)

Approval of the Dissertation Proposal

To progress from writing the proposal to achieving "approval" for the proposal you are likely to accomplish several steps:

* approval by the two- or three-member dissertation committee;
* acceptance by the program faculty; and
* acceptance by an inter-departmental group of faculty.

Your primary focus in seeking approval is your committee, who have expertise in your specific domain, and have worked with you in the formulation of your topic and research questions. Your committee helps you in designing your study. Your committee then has a vested interest in making sure your proposal is "funded" or approved when it gets reviewed by a committee of the program faculty. Thus, they are likely to be very cautious in offering their approval. Their academic standards are open to public scrutiny in your dissertation proposal. They will want to avoid problems with collegial and external reviewers, so their evaluations are likely to be intense. They will look at each word carefully. They will look to see if there is a cohesive organization. They will certainly be concerned with the depth of your knowledge as represented in this document. You are likely to revise your document many times in this process.

Once they have each independently approved your proposal, other faculty are likely to review it as well. Some of these reviewers may be responsible for the "format," others may be concerned with protecting the "human subjects" who may provide the data for your study, while others still may be knowledge-able about your research design and/or research problem. These reviews are all intended to discover potential problems prior to initiating the major study. When recommendations are offered, you need to consult with your committee about your next steps in modifying your proposal.

Ultimately, your proposal is sent to the Office of the Director of Graduate Studies, which accepts the recommendations of these groups, verifying that all the established procedures have been followed. If there are any problems, this Graduate Director facilitates the process for resolving these concerns. Typically, you will receive an official document stating that your dissertation proposal has been "recorded," much like grades are recorded on your official transcript. This document serves as a contract between you and the university, and it also moves you along the path to completing your dissertation. At this stage all of the work you do is towards "writing your dissertation."

Writing Your Dissertation

You have now entered probably the most time-intensive part of the process. You will not only "do your research" but you will also write it up in a form which is acceptable as a dissertation at your institution. You are responsible for doing all the work projected in the proposal. Most of the work will be independently accomplished, initiated by you. Occasionally, faculty meet with you during "office hours" or "program seminars," for example, but these will be at your initiation in the main. Committee members will read and respond to drafts, meet with you, communicate with you on the telephone or via e-mail once you initiate the dialog. Students may create support groups, meeting regularly to offer feedback and encouragement, while sharing resources and experiences. All of these activities are fairly invisible in the university. (For an extended discussion of this process, see Chapters 11–13.)

The next time you "surface" institutionally (aside from semi-annual registrations) is when your oral examination is scheduled. At some point in the process, your chair will decide that she or he is satisfied with what you have completed. After consulting with the reader(s) there will be a decision to "schedule orals." (The student may need to add and/or revise major sections between the time the chair is "ready" and the rest of the committee agrees. "Ready" to one faculty member may mean different things than "ready" to another. "Ready" in one institution may mean different things than in another.) The next big step is the scheduling of the dissertation orals.

In some institutions, the dissertation is written in collaboration with two faculty members, and the selection of the third reader occurs once the chair deems the dissertation ready for this review. Ultimately, all three members must agree to hold the oral examination. Although some consider this step as assurance of passing the orals, or at least guaranteeing a grade of "pass" from these individuals, this is not necessarily the case, as we will see when we address the issue of orals in Chapter 14.

Dissertation Orals

The dissertation committee decides when it is time to schedule orals. The oral examination, often called an oral defense, is a publicly scheduled activity, open to the university community, taking anywhere from one to three hours on average. The participants include, but are not limited to, the dissertation committee, the candidate, and external readers. The outside readers may come from within the university or from institutions nationwide representing expertise in the areas addressed in the dissertation. This last group are considered "outsiders" and are deemed to be likely to be more "objective" in their evaluation. Ultimately, the student wants to "pass." There is usually a written record of the evaluations of the faculty present with a majority of "pass" grades required for the dissertation to be accepted.

There are many academic goals accomplished at the orals: a presentation of the research project, a discussion of the process and findings, and an examination of the candidate's understanding of the dissertation research and the knowledge related to it. There are also power struggles that surface at these events. Depending on the mix of faculty, it is possible to have people whose academic orientations or philosophies are diametrically opposed sitting at the same table. While the committee might represent one clear philosophy, the presence of an opposing voice may provide a contentious setting. If faculty have personal grievances, you may find these evidenced at these events as well.

While at some institutions the orals are a fairly perfunctory experience, with champagne waiting at the conclusion, at other institutions it is fairly common for the student to be assigned to rewrite, rethink, or redo sections of the dissertation. In most instances, while there is a need to continue working on the document, there is no need to go through a second oral examination. (In rare occurrences, the student is required to go through the entire experience again.) Once the dissertation has received a "pass" grade, there is one last hurdle to mount: getting an approved dissertation.

The Approved Dissertation

Although the orals have been successfully completed, your dissertation is not "approved" yet. There is usually a review by an editorial board seeking to confirm that a specific style guide has been followed, and that the dissertation is in a form to be made available to the academic world at large. Some reviews will focus on your format while others consider the effectiveness of your writing style.

After all of these criteria are met, you are almost home free. There are still others who certify that you have paid your tuition for each semester that you have been in the program, and that all library fees and other bureaucratic requirements have been fulfilled. When all of these are satisfied, then your dissertation will be approved, an important element in establishing your eligibility to receive your doctoral degree.

Noncompleters in Doctoral Programs

Approximately 50 per cent of students who enter PhD programs, leave without graduating, according to Barbara Lovitts (1996). This is due to a variety of factors which may be grouped as either *personal* or *programmatic*. Personal factors include: needing time to spend with spouse, children, or ailing parents; having exhausted finances to cover the costs of the program; attention to health; and changing career goals. Programmatic factors include: isolation, confusion, hostility; holding unpopular perspectives or philosophies; and inaccessibility of faculty or courses. Many who leave are embarrassed, feeling defeated by the system. Lovitts identified the lack of institutional support as a major factor in students' decisions to leave. That support could be in the form of information about the program, or in relationships with students and faculty. Those who feel defeated frequently find themselves in another program before long. Being older and wiser, they are more likely to persevere the second or third time around and get their degree.

The whittling down or selection process is a gradual one. At each step there are some who choose not to continue. Some students choose to leave programs rather than to subject themselves to assessment at each of the stages, viewing the process as a game rather than an authentic academic experience.

Concurrent with this evaluation is the student's constant questioning as to whether she or he is ready to subject herself or himself to this process. There are students who decline to be reviewed, thereby removing themselves from the program.

You might wonder why there is this constant evaluation and whittling down of the pool of doctoral students. There are many reasons. From the institution's perspective, there are limited resources available for working on dissertations. There may be a limited number of faculty who are qualified and desire to work on dissertations with doctoral students. Since there appear to be many more doctoral recipients than employment opportunities at universities (e.g. Magner, 1999) the mass media periodically inquire about PhDs being a glut on the market. With limited resources, doctoral students need to be assertive about obtaining the assistance essential for completing the degree.

From the student's perspective, there is little comprehension at the outset of the complexities inherent in writing a dissertation. Many believe they would have been less frustrated and more task-oriented if they knew what to expect in the process. Ultimately all doctoral students benefit from suggestions of strategies for success. From this general overview of the dissertation process, we will now consider some sage advice from current and former doctoral students.

4 Pithy Insights and Suggestions for Success

Figure 4.1 *Some personal advice*
Source: Scott Arthur Maesar, *Chronicle of Higher Education*

*"Your thesis is important, Edward, but you need
to howl once in a while, too!"*

When current and former doctoral students discuss their expectations and experiences in doctoral programs, they offer useful suggestions and perceptions on the dissertation process. Being mindful both that each person's experience is unique, and that people typically experience some ambivalence in this high-stakes endeavor, the range of individual experiences is potentially unchartable. The eighty-five suggestions in this chapter are offered, by students and graduates, to guide you – to help you to avoid problems that others have confronted, or at least to prepare you to avoid being taken by surprise. The suggestions are clustered around six issues:

- dissertation topic selection;
- the dissertation committee;
- organization;
- writing;
- the university community;
- personal stance.

Each suggestion is numbered, to note the different contributors. You will find some reassuring and some daunting. While some may not make any sense at this moment, as you progress, you will probably identify with the range of perspectives represented.

Dissertation Topic Selection

1 Start searching for your dissertation topic with your first course – and your course assignments.
2 I could not find anyone in the department who was willing to work with me on a subject I wanted to research. It was only when I asked to help one of the professors with his research that I was accepted into the "club."
3 Read multiple dissertations – chapter by chapter – as you go through your courses.
4 Find a topic you love. You could be working on it for years.
5 Choose a topic which will have significance to you after you are done.
6 Choose a topic in which you are intensely and independently interested.
7 I wish I had looked for a dissertation topic from the moment I started the program and used the course assignments as an opportunity to explore topics that might have led me towards a dissertation topic.

The Dissertation Committee

8 Find professors with a track record for graduating students.
9 Find a good mentor – a person you respect and can work well with.
10 I worked in isolation and misinterpreted critique as failure.
11 Look on your chair as you ally.
12 While your committee has Chapters 1–3, work on Chapter 4. When they return their chapters, give them the next chapter.
13 Take ownership of your dissertation.
14 If you don't ask for professors' time, professors will assume all is OK. Pester them!
15 "Although I value all I've learned, I wish I had chosen an adviser who was actively involved in research. Then I might have begun to acquire the practical knowledge and skills I'll now need to do the dissertation, and in the future. ... Recognize that the ambivalence and uncertainty you may feel is not unique to you nor necessarily a reflection of your intellectual ability or your ability to successfully complete doctoral study" (Bolig, 1982, pp. 19–23).

16 Ask questions if you do not understand. If you think you understand, state your understanding to assure yourself that you really do.

17 Working with my mentor inspired me to strive to reach my full potential.

18 Submissions were not read in a timely manner, never returned unsolicited.

19 I had to make repeated appointments to actually meet with my first chair, who then retired and moved out of town without contacting me. My second chair did not want to read anything until all the chapters were finished.

20 It was difficult to understand that the role of the mentor was to allow the candidate to grow intellectually through independent study. Schools, even graduate schools, don't nurture this.

21 No experience in my graduate studies prepared me for a dissertation-dialog.

22 I was abandoned by my supposed mentor and had to start from scratch. I had no recourse to the aforementioned abandonment.

23 The tenacity, support, and risk-taking of some faculty is amazing.

24 When my chair referred to me as a "blocked writer" I was astounded. First, that he was talking about me to other students, and then that he thought that I was "blocked." It took me a long time to get beyond that.

25 Find people you trust and enjoy working with.

26 Choose your program and adviser carefully. They will be the difference between finishing and not finishing.

27 Find professors who are interested in helping you succeed.

Organization

28 You will need to be a real researcher. Start early. Join the appropriate professional organizations. Get and read journals. Develop researching skills.

29 Everything important should go into a file or notebook immediately.

30 Make sure all references are complete so none have to be looked up later.

31 Force yourself to write every day, tired or not.

32 Set and meet your own deadlines.

33 Document everything.

34 Never throw anything away.

35 Get the library to support your efforts.

36 Establish *your* agenda, *your* questions as you progress, and what *you* want feedback on.

37 Go through as fast as possible.

38 Get organized – and re-organized – again and again.

39 Expect unplanned diversions. Provide some leeway in your schedule.

40 Make time to smell the roses!

Writing

41 There are professionals who edit dissertations and others who help you work your way through. These people are particularly helpful if you have difficulty getting feedback from your committee.

42 Work section by section and chapter by chapter.

43 I had no idea how long it takes.

44 Never, never accept ABD status. You have invested too much money and energy into this and you need it for future employment. It opens doors.

45 Writing a dissertation is tedious.

46 You can do it. Don't let anyone intimidate you and tell you that you can't do it. Take a few years and focus. Set your priorities and decide to put the rest of your life on hold and go for it.

47 Anything worthwhile requires hard work and dedication.

48 Use a word processor.

49 Set a block of time everyday when you will be undisturbed – to work on your dissertation. It may have to be from 4:00 am to 6:00 am.

50 Learn a variety of software programs conducive to your dissertation, including those which will format according to the required style (e.g. MLA, APA).

51 Get a flat-bed scanner to ease the process.

52 Get your own computer. Don't share.

53 Become familiar with the required format.

54 Expect constant revision – even of revised text.

55 Write every day and commit yourself to doing something towards completion each day.

56 Find a critical reader who will play devil's advocate.

57 You can't over-emphasize the need to save and back up all of your computer records.

58 Keep copies (hard and diskette) in several places.

The University Community

59 Doctoral students are, in a sense, the "children" of their chairs.

60 Look for an institution that prides itself on how it treats people, on the warm relations between faculty and students, and that seems to be peopled by reasonably happy students – instead of looking at prestigious and famous programs. I'd also follow a field and topic that I really loved, instead of picking a field that aligned me with a prestigious advisor. Of course, the irony of this is that once I got the backing of a good institution and a prominent advisor, I have had the freedom to do the work I really wanted to do. If I had not had such "important" support, I'm not sure I'd have been able to get a job. There are lots of nasty ironies and snubbers in academia.

61 The faculty at the university were "by me" when my family and friends weren't.

62 Don't isolate yourself!! And don't allow yourself to be isolated. Create support groups.

63 Create a community. Meet informally with other students who are going through the process and commiserate and encourage each other. If it is possible, collaborate with other students who are working on topics closely related to yours.

64 The fond memories I have mostly focus around the interesting places I went while doing research and the friendly support I received from my student-colleagues as we struggled through our dissertations. Without these sort of "perks" I'd never have finished.

65 Don't make waves – make peace and get done!

66 Be cautious of being perceived as not valuing, or not respecting faculty.

67 Students get sucked into the politics, unwittingly and perhaps even unintentionally.

68 Students who presented proposals were often brought to tears in the process.

69 Graduate faculty were divided on their opinions about student projects.

70 Be realistic: the academic world has as many "bad apples" as the rest of the world. There are many with altruistic values, but most are trying to survive themselves, and thus, not overly concerned with others' survival or growth. There are even a few sickos who seem out to destroy students' self-esteem.

Personal Stance

71 Take pleasure and delight in ideas and in exploration, and in the fact that you have given yourself this wonderful opportunity. Don't let yourself get trapped into rationalizing the process such as calling the process "jumping hurdles" when you get into trouble with your goals.

72 Immerse yourself in your study.

73 Persevere. Select an area you have a strong interest in – and don't give up.

74 When responding to impatient, harassing, inquisitive friends' inquiries about your progress offer:

- I'll graduate when I finish my dissertation.
- When I finish, I'll be done.
- I'm taking my time; I'm really enjoying this.

You could follow this remark with some long-winded explanation of coding data sources or ethnographic recording strategies, and the importance of triangulation. Since they really have no idea what you're talking about, the conversation will revert to other topics.

75 Transcribing my data was the best antidote when my father was sick. I didn't have to think about him while I was transcribing.

76 There comes a point when one must get away from the dissertation altogether.

77 I was amazed at how much I enjoyed doing research on my own. Then, having someone to talk with about my reading and my study was a real high. I discovered I really enjoyed the academic life.

78 Celebrate each accomplishment.

79 Not only are you in it on your own, but you may find that others will seek to make it more difficult for you to accomplish your goal.

80 You need to take on the total responsibility for getting the degree, depending ultimately on no one but yourself.

81 Life gets increasingly complex. Don't put this off.

82 Recognize that this is a major decision – a life-changing decision. It changes the way you are perceived by your friends, relatives, colleagues, and potential employers, as well as yourself.

83 The key is not merely to get through, but to create a foundation for a life-time of important work.

84 Enjoy the experience and view it as a beginning to intellectual develop-ment, not an end in itself.

85 Be circumspect. Keep your own counsel.

These ideas provide a general sense of what to expect. You will find as you go along that you are having the experiences commented on above, and may create a shared code with your student-colleagues, noting, "Well, I guess I just had a ..." Having this secret code will provide some of the needed release of tension, which is essential to get through with your sanity intact!

In addition to your using these code-numbers, you will notice that your conversations are becoming filled with images and metaphors characterizing your experiences. You are now well-equipped with a sense of the total experi-ence. It is time to start writing *your* dissertation!

Part II
Preparing for *Your* Study

5 Identifying Your Dissertation Topic and Your Research Questions

The opportunity to take a topic of importance to me and concentrate on it for extended periods of time – persisting with an idea and seeing how it develops over time – a pure luxury – and I loved it.

I enjoyed doing the review of the literature. I imagined myself a great detective, tracking down leads one after another. Or it was a chain reaction: one article's bibliography would lead to another great source. The best was when I hit the "mother lode," research directly related to what I wanted to do.

Before writing your dissertation, you need to know what you want to research, what you want to learn. A dissertation is expected to "break new ground" for a discipline, and in the process of breaking new ground, you, as the researcher, become proficient at conducting research.

Although a common belief about research is that we do research to confirm or prove our assumptions, this is inaccurate. Rather, research is a process of searching repeatedly, *re*-searching for new insights and a more comprehensive, cohesive, "elegant" theory. There are probably few, if any "truths" – immutable, never-changing facts. Each research project intends to advance our knowledge, getting closer to "truth." All studies are limited by time, if nothing else. Findings from research allow us to make potentially more accurate predictions. But predictions and hypotheses are not guarantees. (See, for example, *Search and re-search*, edited by Brause and Mayher, 1991, for a detailed explanation of these phenomena.)

While each research project contributes to our growing knowledge, there are qualitative differences in research studies. Not all are equally useful: some are poorly conceived and conducted, while others are carefully conceptualized, operationalized, and analyzed. You will need to decide if your study will be "quick and dirty," fulfilling the letter of the requirement, without advancing knowledge, or a serious attempt, at least, to contribute to our academic world. For some, this decision is not easy. Some doctoral students just want to get done. Others hold that if they are spending their time, they want the result to be potentially useful, not merely an academic exercise which will collect dust on a library shelf or use up space in a database when it is finished. Clearly the more time you devote to planning and doing your study, the more likely it will make a contribution to your discipline. Similarly, the less time you devote to thinking about your study, the less likely it will have any impact beyond perhaps qualifying you to receive your degree.

There is another element to consider in this equation: the faculty at your institution. Since, ultimately, some faculty members will need to sign their names as "supporters" of your dissertation, you might find that faculty will not work with you on a topic of little significance. Others may place their emphasis on the doctoral student learning to conduct independent research. Your decision about the tack you will take in doing your dissertation cannot be made in isolation. You need to know about the generally accepted practice in your department and make your decision with this knowledge.

For most, the identification of "what to study" evolves slowly as they become immersed in a variety of concepts, theories, philosophies, and research in the required coursework. Some students enter a program with a clear idea of what they want to do for their dissertation. There are at least two schools of thought about *when* to identify your research focus:

• The *earlier* in your coursework you decide on an area of study the better. You focus all of your attention on the issue, connecting all assignments and readings to your research focus.
• The *later* in the process you decide the better. With this extended knowledge, you are in a position to see where there are gaps and conflicts in your discipline, and you may design a study which will lead to expanding your discipline's knowledge.

Clearly there are benefits and limitations to each perspective. A middle ground is probably most productive, wherein you gradually focus, while maintaining interest in a wide range of potential research areas. Ultimately, the time will arrive when you are "ready."

There are many essential ingredients which contribute to your readiness to start writing your dissertation. Some academic and personal characteristics of doctoral students who are "ready" include:

• a sense of wonder, interest, and/or excitement about a specific topic or question;
• extensive familiarity with "the literature" and the current state of knowledge in the field or discipline of your doctoral program[1];
• encouragement and support for you and your ideas within your program community;
• time to work on the project;
• a desire to contribute to a discipline or field; and
• a determination to complete the doctoral program and go on with your life beyond graduate school.

You might want to assess your own readiness for getting started using the grid presented below. Place a check (✔) next to those items which describe you at this time. Place a minus (–) next to those items which are missing at this time.

Category	Example/potential criteria	Rating (✔ or –)
A sense of wonder, interest, excitement about a specific topic or question	Outline a talk on your topic for a ten-minute presentation	
Extensive familiarity with the "literature" and the current state of knowledge in the field	List ten key references and their main theses	
Encouragement and support for me and my ideas within my program	Name three faculty and three peers who support your interest	
Time to work on the project	Identify a block of time each day when you will work on your dissertation	
A desire to contribute to a discipline or field	Explain the potential impact of your study	
A determination to complete the doctoral program	What will you place on hold while you immerse yourself in your dissertation? Do you have plans for "after dissertation?"	

Now that you've noted your current status on these six characteristics, you need to consider and respond to that evaluation. If at least three items are checked, you're probably ready. If less than three are checked, you'll need to consciously work on establishing your readiness before proceeding. In the ideal world, if *all* items had checks next to them, you would progress very rapidly. In the real world, we try to have as many of these issues covered as we can. Clearly you cannot do this project alone. It takes a large number of people working with you to accomplish this!

Ironically, doctoral students frequently sabotage their own progress, allowing others to control their academic advancement. Our lives become increasingly complex and integrated into others' lives as we take on additional responsibilities. This factor alone makes it difficult for an adult to isolate herself or himself for any extended period of time. Getting done with the dissertation usually takes obsessive dedication, with the dissertation becoming the most important activity in a person's life for a finite time. This observation suggests that the sooner you start, and the more rapidly you progress, the more likely you are to graduate. There are advantages to moving quickly: the research you have read in your coursework remains current, the faculty interested in your research questions are ready to work with you; your questions continue to intrigue you and your responsibilities to others are manageable. Knowing what is likely to be expected at each stage of the process of dissertation writing will enable you to take charge of this activity in your life.

Creating a Setting for Working on Your Dissertation

While there are multiple ways to work on a dissertation, there are three typical ways to get started, as represented graphically in Figure 5.1:

- working independently;
- working collaboratively with other students in your program; and
- working in consultation with faculty in your program.

Your working environment could take many forms. Let's consider the advantages and disadvantages of some.

Working Independently

You are totally in control when you are working independently. You set the time, you set the pace, you set the focus, you critique your work, you decide when it's ready for external review. If you are a self-starter, this might be a good model. If you get easily discouraged and then stop working, this will not be a good setting for you. If you have more confidence in your own views than in anyone else's, you will not be sidetracked by potentially differing perspectives. If you are good at reflecting on your work, finding where your text is unclear, and where additional resources are needed, for example, then working independently may be a good setting for you. Being familiar with your own working style, you will be in an excellent position to decide if this setting will be productive for you.

Figure 5.1   *Creating your working environment: one set of options*

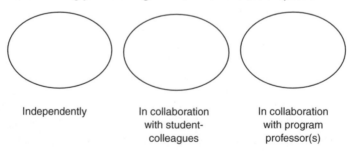

| Independently | In collaboration with student-colleagues | In collaboration with program professor(s) |

Collaborating with Student-colleagues

Collaboration can take several forms. You could restrict your group to include only student-colleagues who are in your program, for example, or you could create a more expansive group, drawing on doctoral students across many programs at your university or including colleagues from your workplace. You could also restrict your group to one or two other people. Or you could have a relatively large group of seven or eight. Your comfort level, your experiences working in groups, and your familiarity with other students in the program will all contribute to the form of this collaborative group. The size of the group and the frequency of the meetings may vary over time as group members progress or get diverted to other projects.

When you collaborate with others, you determine mutually agreeable times and places to work. You start and stop in collaboration with others. You progress at a rate comfortable for those in your group. Your advancement will be monitored by your group, and facilitated or restricted by them. In a collaborative group, your knowledge is enriched by sharing with your collaborators. When the experiences and expertise of all the members in the group contribute to the progress of each participant, a collaborative setting is useful. Each member in such a setting must know or learn to be a productive collaborator, helping others while reciprocally obtaining the assistance needed.

At times, group members have been known to cater totally to others' views, reluctant to take a stand, perhaps unsure of their own grounding. These individuals may be more interested in harmony than in learning or exposing their own thinking to others' analyses. Or they may have little confidence in their own thinking, deferring to others' ideas almost automatically. If you choose to work in a collaborative group, monitor and evaluate the effects of your participation on the evolution and completion of your work.

Collaborating with Program Professor(s)

Knowing that ultimately the dissertation will need to be accepted by the program professor(s), doctoral students frequently identify one or two professors to guide their progress. They depend exclusively on these faculty members to direct them to appropriate readings, to tell them when and what to write or revise, and when and where to do their data collection, for example. In this scenario, a student may be overly influenced by the biases and preferences of the professor regarding differences in opinion in the discipline or field. The student might become something of a clone of the professor, depending on the styles of the professor and the student. A student may also have easier access to many developing ideas in the field, and perhaps, unpublished works as well, when collaborating with a professor who is actively researching in the field of specialization. Clearly the student in this setting knows how at least one professor will respond to the work which she or he is doing, and knows where to revise, where to elaborate, and when to get ready for public presentation.

Since the faculty member has more power than the student in the college setting, the professor-as-colleague is not a truly collaborative arrangement.

Each of these settings offers many advantages to the doctoral student. They also present potential obstacles to completion. Consequently, we need to think of alternative settings. We can contemplate breaking down the isolation in each potential arrangement, and finding ways to utilize these settings, choosing different groupings to accomplish specific tasks. You might start in one setting and then move back and forth among settings. When all three are available to you, you are likely to find the most productive environment (see Figure 5.2).

There are many places where you might choose to start. You need to create the settings which will expedite your progress.

Identifying Your Research Problem or Question

You may have a burning desire to try a study similar to one you've read, but with older students, or in a different setting. It is crucial in the process of selecting a topic that you choose one which is exciting to you. If the topic is not intriguing to you, experience tells us that you are not likely to be able to get up the energy to work on it independently at 4:00 am on a Sunday morning, for instance. Thus, the place to start is to find a topic which is of keen interest to you personally and professionally. Now you may ask, "How do I find that topic?" You may consider some options, for example:

1   You draw on the knowledge which you acquired in your coursework and from your independent reading and journal writing.

Figure 5.2   *Creating your working environment: an alternative view*

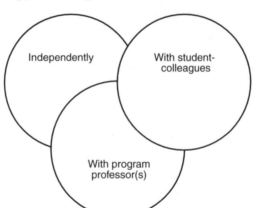

2   You engage in dialogs with professors about topics which might be accept-
    able, knowing your dissertation will only get done with the assistance and
    support of the faculty.
3   You collaborate with student-colleagues, discussing the topics they are
    contemplating for their research, using recently accepted dissertations as
    samples of what your dissertation needs to represent, as well as sites where
    recommendations for future research are presented.
4   You draw on your personal and professional experiences.

The implicit expectation of a doctoral program is that students will engage in
extended inquiry, maintaining an open mind about the conflicting theories and
perspectives advanced by the leaders in the field. Many students at the end of
the required coursework have questions that interest them, questions which
could ultimately be phrased as research questions. Let's consider a variety of
effective ways to move the agenda from several potential topics which might be
interesting to explore to identifying *your* specific research question. I encourage
you to consider all these strategies, and then create a process that is most
compatible with your personal learning style.

    A first step is to identify some potential questions which you might want to
research for your dissertation. You might find it useful at this point to note
some of the topics and questions which interest you. Putting these ideas on
paper will help you to progress.

Potential questions or issues to consider

1   How does the computer influence student writing in college?

2

3

4

Now that you've listed some potential questions, you will need to consider several issues. Some criteria for evaluating these were suggested by Hawley (1993):

- Is it interesting to me?
- Is it manageable?
- Is it within the range of my competence?
- Is the data source reliable?
- Does it make a significant and original contribution?
- Is it [too] controversial?

(Hawley, 1993, pp. 41–6)

Review each of the potential questions you've listed above using Hawley's criteria as a basis for either revising or eliminating each from your pool of potential questions. You may also want to add to this list.

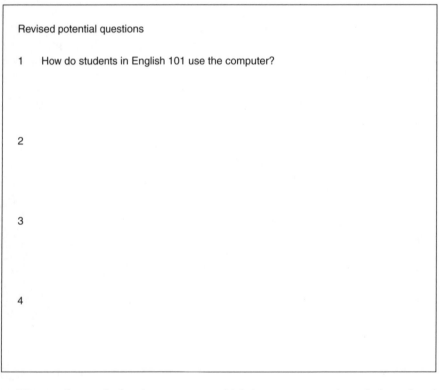

Revised potential questions

1   How do students in English 101 use the computer?

2

3

4

Now you're ready for the next step, which is to note your knowledge related to each of the revised questions. Use the form below to organize your notation of the major theorists, research studies, etc., which might help to inform your research for each question. This is not a simple task. You might find it useful to work intensively on this grid. You might identify a large number of issues and connect these issues to the readings you've done in your courses. After you've exhausted your knowledge, you might brainstorm with some colleagues to expand the resources, refine the questions, and remind yourself of additional sources of information.

Revised questions	Theories and research related to the topic
1 How do students in English 101 use the computer?	• Development of writing proficiencies • Relationship between writing and learning • Relationship between reading and writing • Adult learning
2	
3	
4	

As you progress, you are likely to identify some gaps in your knowledge. Depending on the outcome of this self-assessment, you may want to consider your options. For example:

• Is this really an unexplored issue?
• How can I rephrase the question to tap into my knowledge?
• Are there topics more closely related to my knowledge?
• Do I know anyone who has conducted research in a similar area?
• Will the study help in my professional responsibilities? ... or in my future career?

You will find it useful to identify resources which might contribute to your understanding as a way to move the project along, drawing on related databases which you know are available, even if you've never used them. In addition, you might try to rephrase your questions more precisely, recognizing that each question must be highly focused guiding a research project that is "do-able" and do-able in a reasonable time. For example, a question such as "What strategies do good readers use when reading *King Lear*?" might be revised to inquire: "What strategies do 12th grade students whose standardized reading scores place them in the top quartile of their grade nationally report using when reading *King Lear*?"

Questions and issues which intrigue me	What I know about the topic	Potential additional resources to address the topic
1		
2		
3		
4		

As you share this list with a trusted friend, you may fill in more information. Then you are ready to share it with a professor or two as a way to initiate a conversation about your dissertation. At times, students became concerned that others will steal their research questions and are reluctant to talk about their plans. In such settings it is essential to be circumspect in all your conversations.

Alternative Starting Points

Another way to start could involve identifying the topics which have intrigued you. Then, "push the envelope" by identifying related, unexplored, or controversial issues.

A third strategy might be to list some questions which are generated from your personal experiences (at home, at work, at the market, at the theater), and then connect your potential exploration of these topics with the knowledge you have acquired and the disciplines which you have explored in your courses.

A fourth approach might be to review your journal writing or file for "potential research," noting the numerous questions you posed as you reflected on your personal learning throughout your coursework. These questions have the potential to lead you to an exciting research question.

A final suggestion might find you conferring with program professors, brainstorming possible topics, particularly ones which might be aligned with their current research agenda. Many university *Bulletins* list faculty research interests. By studying the faculty's interests, for example, you can start formulating a tentative list of areas which interest you while using the information to seek out publications written by these faculty. By becoming more knowledge-

Intriguing topics/issues	A different perspective
1	1
2	2
3	3
4	4

able about the faculty's work, you are able to obtain a useful direction for your own research.

You do not start by "writing your dissertation." You start by identifying a problem. You may write notes as a process towards clarifying your questions. These notes may become useful as you advance to the stage of writing your formal dissertation. You will probably write many pages prior to actually writing text which will become part of your completed dissertation.

The crucial issue is not so much *where* you start as much as *that* you start. Start by reading, or by talking with colleagues, or by asking professors about potential topics you are considering. But start! The sooner you start, the sooner you are likely to get done. Once you have a sense of what you might want to research, you are ready to consider forming your dissertation committee.

Note

1 This is usually acquired through reading journal articles and books, as well as, for example, attending lectures and conference presentations.

6 Forming Your Dissertation Committee

I realized that getting along with people was even more important than being academically talented.

I really enjoyed being a student. If I had this attitude during my undergraduate years, it would have been a better experience. Perhaps maturity does have its advantages.

The process of identifying your dissertation committee is probably the most significant decision you will make in your program. Before suggesting criteria for selecting your committee, we need to understand the roles and responsibilities of the committee.

The Dissertation Committee Structure

The university establishes the doctoral committee structure as a vehicle to guide the student from course work to doctoral orals. The purpose of the dissertation committee is twofold: from the university's perspective the faculty are expected to assure the maintenance of the tacit "standards" of the university. From the student's perspective, the faculty are the teachers guiding the student in developing a dissertation. This is a true apprenticeship model.

The dissertation committee becomes the group of faculty responsible for your progress from the identification of your research question through your dissertation oral examination. The development of your dissertation proposal, your data collection and analysis, and documentation of your study in the form of a dissertation are activities which evolve over time, consuming at least two years, and frequently considerably longer. Thus, it is essential that your committee work well together and with you.

Typically there are two or three faculty members who comprise a dissertation committee. These faculty have different responsibilities within the group. One person has the title of chair, mentor, director, or head (for a listing of these common titles, see Figure 3.1). The others are called "readers." The hierarchical organization established with this naming connotes differential status and responsibility among the faculty. The chair has the major task of guiding the student from vague idea to dissertation orals. The chair is assisted by other faculty, all contributing to the development of an acceptable dissertation. The chair collaborates with the readers in determining when the dissertation is ready for orals, but the readers expect the chair to be the major advisor in the research process.

Since most doctoral students are hazy in their understanding of most of these stages, they usually depend on their committee to provide the needed information or to refer them to appropriate resources. Ideally, the doctoral committee is comprised of faculty with different areas of expertise, who will contribute to the completion of your dissertation. For example, one member might be expert in research design, another in the current theories prevailing in a discipline, and a third in analytical processes. You will tap these resources many times in the process of working on your dissertation.

Each committee is virtually an independent entity. It functions in isolation from others in the university deciding when the dissertation proposal is ready for public evaluation, and, ultimately, when the dissertation is ready for public scrutiny. "Going public" involves reviews by external readers, editors, the department chair, and others who are either responsible for or interested in evaluating specific aspects of the dissertation. Thus, the committee guides the doctoral student in this whole process.

You may call your committee your "doctoral committee," your "committee," or your "dissertation committee." You only have one committee, but these terms are used interchangeably (see Figure 3.1). Over the years, the faculty in your academic program and your university developed an implicit under-standing of what is expected in the process of completing a dissertation. These faculty are the ones who will, in the main, become members of your dissertation committee.

In most instances, faculty have the choice to accept or decline the invitation to serve on a doctoral committee. (In some institutions, the chair is appointed without consulting the student. If this is the practice in your institution, you may proceed to the next chapter where we consider effective procedures for working with your committee.) It is not unusual to see the same names on multiple dissertation committees. Faculty with similar expertise and expecta-tions are happy to sponsor students who are working with their colleagues. Others, impressed with the student's work in different courses, seek to work with the student on the dissertation. Some of the reasons faculty choose to work on dissertation committees include:

- to influence the future directions of their discipline;
- to help students get done with their doctoral programs;
- to be surrounded by the "youth" of the academic world;
- to obtain status by working with the most advanced students in the depart-ment; and/or
- to fulfill university responsibilities.

You select your committee from among those in your department and related departments, those whose courses you've taken, and those whose work bears on the focus of your dissertation. Some of these faculty may be members of other programs or other schools within your university. In rare cases, experts from beyond the university are chosen. Successful committees have predictable characteristics which you may want to consider. For example, their members are:

- cooperative and respectful of each other;
- knowledgeable in the discipline;
- familiar with the procedures of the university;
- effective at reflecting on student work and promoting student learning;
- stable, responsible professionals, reasonably responsive to student needs; and
- supportive of student progress, returning work in a timely manner.

You probably have several choices of faculty from your program who may be appropriate. But some are likely to be easier for you to talk to. Some are eager to work with you. You will need to work through these choices, focusing on which people are going to help *you* to get done!

At times, students have difficulty finding any faculty who are willing to work with them. This might be a reflection of tension in the academy. It may indicate different priorities than your own. It may suggest that the faculty think you will be difficult to work with or will require inordinate attention and assistance or the program may be in the process of being phased out. You have a few choices to consider at this juncture:

- Request assistance from your department chair.
- Request assistance from the Dean of Students or the Director of Graduate Studies.
- Revise your research focus.
- Leave the program.

Each person has a unique experience. These variations in experience are sometimes considered part of the "dance" which is choreographed as you work your way through to your dissertation and beyond. Some say this is just like life in general. There are multiple paths we may each travel, different dances we may each prefer.

Characteristics to Consider in Selecting your Committee Chair

David Brown, in an interview about his experiences writing an undergraduate thesis, noted:

> A good thesis advisor should be knowledgeable about your subject and should be familiar with what your particular department expects. ... However, it is even more important that your advisor is willing to spend hours helping you improve your thesis and is someone with whom you can

establish a good rapport. ... Enduring the criticism of an advisor with whom you do not get along well is likely to breed resentment.

(Brown, 1997, p. 2)

Rosemary Bolig offers additional advice:

Each student will need the kind of committee that can demand of her the quality of work she is capable of producing. Each student will also need a committee that can be firm and supportive and give her the kind of encouragement often needed in this final stage of the doctoral experience.

(Bolig, 1982, p. 24)

Professors are human beings, representing the same range of good and bad players as is evident in all other settings, including politics, medicine, law, and commerce. Some seek to work with students with limited confidence, keeping them dependent. Others seek to empower their students, sharing experiences and nurturing their growing understanding of the academic world along with their independence as researchers and academics. Some of these personal traits may be attributed to the professor's tenure status at the university.

Untenured faculty tend to be less sure of their own longevity at the institution, and may prefer to restrict the number of graduates who may eventually compete with them for posts. This stance might be evidenced in their delaying student progress and discouraging student creativity. Others, looking to retirement soon, may be reluctant to take on new students, concerned that they will retire prior to the students' completion of their dissertations. Others may prefer to dedicate their time to their own research, choosing to work only with students who either are willing to work on the professor's research, or need no assistance. And so the dance of selecting a chair and a dissertation committee is far from easy for the doctoral student. The more information you have about the individual faculty, the easier it will be for you to make a decision about which individuals may both potentially agree to work with you and help you to achieve your goals.

Some additional criteria to consider in selecting your chair:

- Interaction style which is compatible with your own. Some may prefer to provide feedback on written drafts, with little dialog. Others may choose to read and evaluate text collaboratively. Some feedback may be vague (e.g. "Redo this section"), while others may provide detailed comments (e.g. "You need to identify the three main issues and then critique them in light of the other theories you have discussed"). Some may ask questions without offering any assistance. Others may give explicit assignments with guidelines for completion, while others may say, "Get started and let me know how you're doing." Some may wish to see you weekly while others may be happy only when responding to polished text.
- Knowledge of the discipline of your dissertation. If your chair shares your strong interest in your topic, she or he will be in a position to apprise you of unpublished work in progress, as well as important published resources.

You will need to respect the knowledge of your chair, who is likely to criticize your work, requiring you to revise texts, for example. You will need to value and feel comfortable with the way in which feedback and criticism are provided.

- Time to work with you as you progress. Since faculty are fairly independent in scheduling appointments, you will need to identify faculty who will make time in their schedules to work with you. A related element is the university status of the faculty. Whereas untenured faculty contracts may not be renewed, tenured faculty are likely to be more stable. Faculty who leave one institution frequently elect to continue working with their doctoral students, but these arrangements get to be more complex. Sabbatical leaves also potentially interrupt progress. You will need to consider the relative stability and accessibility of faculty along with your own time constraints and projections.
- Success at bringing students to graduation. Since you are concerned with completing your degree, you will want to work with someone who has a fairly consistent record of success with students finishing their dissertations. Some students seek to be connected with the "stars" in the department, with people who are well-known internationally. Star-status, however, may contribute to students' difficulty in meeting "standards," or in finding time to meet with them when they are on the conference circuit. On the other hand, their national status might facilitate inclusion at prestigious professional conferences.
- Nurturing students in the academic tradition. The professor must be comfortable in initially leading, but eventually freeing, students to become independent researchers. At first, the student is dependent on the chair and the committee, but eventually the student should be perceived as an expert and a colleague. If the professor is a confidence-booster for the student, the student may find it easier to progress.
- Personal preference. Some students prefer to work with female faculty, while others prefer to work with male faculty. Some prefer older people, while others younger.

It is unlikely that you will find all the characteristics of the perfect mentor in one person. You will need to identify the one or two characteristics that you consider to be essential for the person who will guide your apprenticeship. It is likely that other members of your committee will be able to offer different strengths which "round out" your committee. You certainly want your committee to be supportive of your progress.

Selecting the Chair of Your Dissertation Committee

Each student selects the dissertation chair. You will discover a subtle process in which faculty implicitly or explicitly make known an interest in working with you. As a way of indicating interest in serving as the chair of your committee, a faculty member may inquire who your dissertation chair is. If you respond that you do not have one yet, they may volunteer to fill that void. If you indicate that you are not sure what your topic is yet, they may seek to engage you in conversation to guide that selection.

The fact that a faculty member has engaged you in this discussion suggests a respect for the quality of your academic work. If no one has approached you, however, that is not a reason to be depressed. Perhaps they are unaware of how far you have progressed in your program, or perhaps they think you have already selected your chair. You may need to initiate the conversation and the process. (If a faculty member approaches you, you need not think that person is your only opportunity. Try to be in charge of this process without conveying a sense of arrogance. You may talk with many faculty, letting each know you are *exploring* topics, gathering information before deciding on your committee at this moment.)

Students sometimes approach a faculty member. They may ask the professor if she or he has time to take on another doctoral student. It is useful to have a draft of an idea, or to request time to talk about possible areas of research. It is important to let the professor know where you are in the process of working on your dissertation.

You probably do not want to ask a professor blithely to accept such a crucial role in your doctoral program without knowing more about how successfully the two of you can work together. So you might be wise to indicate that you are in the process of thinking about a topic and want additional insights. Along with sharing perspectives on your proposed research problem, you will get a sense of how you may work with this individual on a long-term basis. Along with your personal interactions with different professors, use as much "insider information" as you can: ask other doctoral students about their experiences and knowledge of different people; and read dissertations they have sponsored. Remember to access multiple data sources, not limiting yourself to one perspective. It is reassuring to have confirming information on the inferences you are drawing from your inquiries. (Never under-estimate the power of the university gossip mill. Get information you can trust.)

Faculty may make themselves hard to find to avoid giving an explicit "turn down." Given the voluntary nature of chairing a dissertation committee, faculty typically elect to work with the candidates they perceive to be the strongest academically and the easiest to work with. Students who demonstrate these characteristics in their coursework are frequently sought after by faculty.

In the process of considering your options from among your program faculty, you will want to identify as clearly as you can what your hopes are in working with a faculty member as the chair of your dissertation committee. Some issues you might consider include:

* Do you have confidence that Professor X can help/guide you?
* Are you ready to accept direction and criticism from Professor X?
* Are you willing to adapt to Professor X's interaction style?

You need to identify the best match between your learning style and the faculty who are available to work with you. Be open-minded in your exploration. Sometimes faculty are different in one-to-one relationships than they are in lectures or seminar classes. In your exploration you may find a professor working on a project that interests you. This might be a combination made in heaven. Consider it carefully. For each student the response is probably different. (Some like to be told exactly what to do, while others want to learn how to think on their own.) Selecting your committee is not easy but it is essential for you to progress. Do not expect perfection. There probably is no such thing as a perfect committee – or a perfect doctoral student for that matter!

In this process of selecting the members of your committee you want to be cautious of offending others in the department, those who will be your professional colleagues once you graduate and/or those who may ultimately participate in the process of evaluating your dissertation. You never know which committee members will need to be replaced, which colleagues will participate in your oral defense as "outside readers," or which will be in positions to derail your progress.

You want to keep everyone's friendship and respect. This requires very careful planning. Keep your eye on your goal and avoid participation in any intrigues or gossip which may place you in one political camp or another. (Although you may have been oblivious to the political nature of the academic world as you work with them in a group, you are likely to become increasingly cognizant of the internal frictions and even wars which prevail in most departments. Several fascinating books on this topic are included in Appendix C.) As a doctoral student you are well advised to remove yourself from internal political discussions. Make it very clear to yourself and the faculty in your department that you do not want to become involved. You want to get *done*! You have an agenda that keeps you very busy, and there's no time in your calendar for gossiping or for politics.

While it will be inevitable that some faculty might feel rejected because you have not asked them to chair your committee, you may still maintain a professional relationship, inquiring about their work and acknowledging how their courses helped in your dissertation work. At all times convey a sense of respect for all, while progressing on your own work. Expect to have tense times, but also expect to find ways to work through these. Most people have.

Selecting the Readers on Your Doctoral Committee

The readers on your committee work with your chair to promote your progress. They may work with you at other times than your chair, drawing on different areas of strength. Some may only read drafts which have been approved by your chair. They may offer recommendations which need to be considered in collaboration with your chair. Your chair is the leader in this process, so make sure you follow your chair's advice on how to proceed at all times. Ultimately, your readers and your chair must approve your dissertation proposal, and eventually your dissertation.

Working in collaboration with your chair, you will select appropriate readers. You will want faculty who can work well together, and your chair will be in the best position to determine these collegial relationships. You may offer some suggestions, but you should allow your chair to guide you in this decision. The committee will stay with you, guiding your apprenticeship. In some institutions this committee evolves during the writing of the proposal as the needed expertise becomes evident. In other institutions, the committee may grow from the time of the proposal to the completed dissertation. Find out what the process is at your university.

You will talk with the members of your committee as you develop your dissertation proposal, as you conduct your research, and as you write your dissertation. We will address these relationships in the next chapter.

7 Roles and Responsibilities of Dissertation Committees

> Be determined. Set your goal. Save the money (at least as much as you can); get
> a supportive mentor who is knowledgeable with your topic. Go for it. Finish.
> Don't stay ABD.

> I was wiser than I thought.

The formal establishment of your committee usually happens simultaneously
with the university's official approval of your proposed dissertation research.
(This document is typically called your "dissertation proposal.") In the time
between completing your courses and having an approved dissertation proposal
you will work with faculty who are likely to become the officially designated
committee. You may consider them your "unofficial" or your "proposed"
committee for the time being. But they are not yet your official committee.
There are no temporary titles which are generally used around the university, so
we will use the terms "chair" and "reader," understanding that these are potential roles and titles which may change in the process of developing your
dissertation proposal.

During the time when you are drafting your dissertation proposal you may
consult with a large number of professors. This process is both a testing ground
for your ability to work well as a committee and the beginning of the road to
writing your dissertation. Once the chair and readers have agreed that your
dissertation proposal is done, they initiate a process within the university,
simultaneously accomplishing two important official steps:

- appointing your dissertation committee; and
- accepting your dissertation proposal.

Because the writing of the dissertation proposal includes the development and
refinement of the research focus, there are likely to be revisions in your
thinking and in the thinking of the faculty who are considering working with
you on your dissertation. You are also likely to find that some faculty, who
might have the expertise, do not make time to talk with you. Simultaneously
you will find others who are both more responsive and have the expertise to
contribute to your proposal. The proposal writing time, then, is a time for the

student to consult with faculty as potential committee members, and for the faculty to consider the best use of their collective and individual time. When your dissertation proposal is accepted, your committee is officially designated. The proposed faculty committee both supports your proposal for approval and advances the approval of their membership on your dissertation committee.

University Concerns

The university is concerned that the faculty who are assigned to a specific committee represent the appropriate areas of expertise needed to conduct the research described in the proposal. In many respects, the university is serving in the role typically taken by funding authorities when deciding whether to support one project over another. Both sponsoring groups have a responsibility to safeguard the scholarly standards of the academic community, approving the intellectual rigor of the committee to supervise the conduct of the research. The committee has a clear charge: to conduct a specific research project, one which utilizes the faculty's established expertise. The committee and the project are thus carefully crafted to be interdependent. The university is delegating responsibility for the scholarly integrity of the project to specific faculty, those the university recognizes as having the appropriate expertise.

The University's Commitment to your Dissertation Work

When you form your dissertation committee, *you* are tacitly committing to writing your dissertation and to completing your doctoral work. And this is a two-way relationship. The establishment of a dissertation committee under the aegis of the university marks an official contract between the doctoral student and the university, identifying specific faculty who will invest their expertise and time in your apprenticeship. This is a major step in your progress toward your doctoral degree. It does not happen casually. The university is virtually entering into a legal contract, naming you as the doctoral student/researcher, working with specific faculty to complete a specific project. The university agrees to support your academic work on this project by delegating this responsibility to specific faculty. In some cases the university will restrict your discussion of your project to within the university until it is completely approved by the university (after doctoral orals). This control of information is intended to protect the student and the university while your research is in progress.

Committee members may change, but not easily.[1] The topic of your dissertation may change, but not easily.[2] This contract is taken seriously by the university and the student. It is the committee's responsibility to maintain the standards of the university when directing your work on your dissertation. It is your responsibility to conduct the proposed research as outlined in the proposal.

During the time when you are "working on your dissertation" you will be moving through many stages in the process of completing your doctoral program. Some of the activities you will engage in during the time labeled "working on my dissertation" include: creating your committee, writing your dissertation proposal, conducting your dissertation research, and preparing for your dissertation orals. The process involves a gradual transformation from apprentice to experienced, independent researcher.

Thinking of your work on your dissertation as similar to an independent study project rather than any other academic activity will be useful. When enrolled in an independent study course, for example, the student is usually responsible for initiating the process, obtaining feedback on work completed, and seeking additional direction in continuing the project. When you are enrolled in an independent study course, you create your own schedule and work space. Although you may feel isolated, you are neither totally alone nor independent. There is a faculty member who is guiding your work. Additionally, you are constantly held to explicit or tacit university standards. It is perhaps useful to consider independent study experiences as transitions or bridges to the doctoral committee structure. Whether working on an independent course or on your dissertation, you are required to initiate the project and to respond to professors' guidance and directives.

The traditional stages in your doctoral program from admission to graduation, with a note of the typical length of time dedicated to each stage, are noted in Table 7.1. Typically, the stages numbered 5–8 are considered times when you are "working on your dissertation." All the time you are working on your dissertation you are working with your committee.

When working on your dissertation, your community changes from collaborating with student-colleagues on the same project in a course to working individually with a faculty committee on a unique project. Although you and the faculty are "working together" on your dissertation, the work that each person does is specialized. The roles of the faculty in this project are to support, facilitate, direct, and evaluate your learning, whereas the student's role is to learn, research, speculate, and write. And there is a major transition during the process wherein the student takes on increasing responsibility for decision-making as the professor(s) relinquish control, enabling the student to become an independent researcher.

The faculty's role changes from being knowledgeable about all aspects of your research to being most knowledgeable about university practice, while the doctoral student changes from a neophyte to an experienced researcher, becoming an expert in one research project. This gradual transition is represented in Figure 7.1. The transformation typically results in the creation of a collaborative team with each member sharing different expertise – the setting for the conversation at the oral defense. Clearly this transition takes time, a period during which you will converse extensively with your committee.

Table 7.1 *The academic stages in the doctoral process*

Individual student's action	Institutional response	Typical time range
Application Phase		
Stage 1 Apply for admission	Admit with provisional matriculation	6 months
Coursework Phase		
Stage 2 Complete some coursework	Admit to Permanent Matriculation	12–18 months
Stage 3 Complete all coursework	Record grades on transcript	12–18 months
Examination Phase		
Stage 4 Pass qualifying exam	Admit to doctoral candidacy	6–12 months
Dissertation Phase		
Stage 5 Select dissertation topic, chair, and committee	Appoint committee	6 months
Stage 6 Draft dissertation proposal	Approve dissertation proposal	12–36 months
Stage 7 Conduct, analyze, and write-up dissertation study	Schedule orals	12–36 months
Stage 8 Prepare for orals	Pass orals	2 months
Revise dissertation	Approve dissertation	1 month
File for graduation	Issue diploma	

Starting to Work with Your Committee

The relationship between you and your dissertation committee is perhaps the most significant factor in your completion of the doctoral degree. It is in your best interest to find ways to make this relationship harmonious and productive. The committee organization requires you to utilize a different set of interaction skills than you used when taking courses. The faculty probably have a history of collaborating in different ways. Although you may have worked with each professor productively, you probably worked with each individually, or only as a member of a whole class. Now that you are an official group, your relationship with each of the professors changes, as do their relationships with you.

Early on it is important to understand the rules for working collaboratively

Figure 7.1 *From dissertation proposal to dissertation: transition in responsibility and expertise*

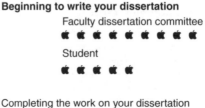

Beginning to write your dissertation
Faculty dissertation committee

Student

Completing the work on your dissertation
Faculty dissertation committee

Student

 = relative responsibility in decision-making

and dialogically. Although it would be idealistic to create an equal relationship, reality reveals that this is not the case. The student usually conforms to the styles of the professors. While there may be some negotiation of procedures for progressing, the professors usually set the rules. And each professor has idiosyncrasies which doctoral students eventually learn to accommodate, or they elect to work with other faculty.

Working with Your Chair

You start with the professor whom you've identified as most likely to be able to help you to complete this project. This professor may prefer you to focus your research questions and write some rationale for your study before asking other faculty to consider serving as readers on your committee. You will write drafts of what might become Chapter 1 of your proposal, considering such issues as how your study will add to current knowledge in your discipline or how it will enlighten some conflicts in the field. The writing that you are being asked to do requires you to focus on a highly targeted issue.

You now need to engage in an in-depth study to determine what is already known, so that your research is not "reinventing the wheel." Your research must build on what has preceded you. The only way you are in a position to advance that issue authoritatively is by knowing the "literature" of your field. Thus, the request for some written text will require extensive reading along with documentation of your understanding. Your writing will accomplish four essential processes:

• You will acquire a depth and breadth of knowledge in your chosen field.

- You will note similarities and contradictions among the theories you learned in separate courses, as you develop your persuasive argument for conducting your planned research.
- You will become aware of the issues which are clear to you and those which are still hazy as you seek to write cohesive drafts of text for your chair.
- You will receive evaluation and feedback on the comprehensiveness of your thinking and the clarity of your writing from the drafts you present.

There are likely to be multiple drafts of this document, with each draft reflecting a refined and intensified understanding of important issues.

While you are writing these drafts, you are also learning the genre of dissertation writing as it is acceptable at your university or as it conforms to the style of writing acceptable in professional publications in your discipline. Frequently students find they need to learn a new writing style. As you read widely in your field, you are becoming immersed in the writing style(s) as well as the concepts. Your writing and conversations with student-colleagues and faculty about your readings will promote your developing proficiency in writing academic discourse.

Thus, although the request that you "write up your research question" may sound simple, it is really quite demanding. Working with your chair, you will learn how to move through this process. With a clear focus, expansive knowledge, and time devoted to your project, you are likely to move through this process very rapidly.

Your chair will probably want you to defer talking with other potential committee members until you have a text that is highly focused, reflects a significant understanding of complex issues, and accommodates the institution's format requirements. You will eventually create a fairly polished text which your chair will accept. This process becomes an initiation into what will be expected of you.

Many students find it simplifies matters to work through the specific research focus with just one professor, and then add perspectives to the discussion once the topic is identified. With a clearly written document in hand, you are prepared to visit with potential committee members. Faculty make judgments about student work from these drafts. Your written drafts and your personal presentation will offer clues about your enthusiasm for the project and your proficiency, for example in writing, following directions, articulating issues and conceptualizing. These characteristics will contribute to faculty members' decisions to serve on your committee. Expect that your readers will offer suggestions which are likely to enhance your study, necessitating additional revisions of your proposal. *Look on all of your work as a work in progress, thereby reducing your anxiety level of seeking a perfect document as a first draft.*

Early on you may initiate conversations with your chair about who might be good readers, when you should talk with them, and what you might bring with you. Once your chair gives the "go ahead," you will need to make an appointment with the professor(s), indicating the intent of your visit. You may be definitive: "I'm hoping you will agree to be on my committee and I have some text I'd like you to read." On the other hand, you may be more circumspect, waiting to see what a professor's reaction is to your ideas, or the way in which you are treated before making any formal request. It is difficult, but not impossible to rescind an invitation to be on your committee. Ask advice from your chair and from student-colleagues who may have experiences to share with you.

Working with your Readers

The readers on your committee support and supplement the directions and guidance offered by the chair of your committee. They are likely to have different viewpoints and perspectives from your chair. When there are conflicting opinions among the members of the committee, it is useful to have three-way or four-way conversations. Traditionally, the chair negotiates differences among the faculty, with the student participating in this process, offering theories and practice which guide the decisions. Make note of the questions and issues addressed in these meetings, as they are likely to recur in other settings, such as at your oral defense.

Seek advice from your chair concerning when to talk with the readers. Some chairs like to limit your interaction with the readers while others prefer that you work as much as possible with the readers. Some readers will only read text that has been approved by the chair and will only meet with you once your chair has approved a significant part of your proposal or your dissertation.

In the process of working with all these faculty members you have access to a rich treasure trove of academic expertise. Try to learn as much as possible from these professors during this time. Ask them about conferences you might attend and publications which might be of value to you. From an academic perspective, this is a utopian experience since you have the assistance of a group of academics pooling their accumulated expertise to promote the success of *your* project. Enjoy it!

By working continuously on your research and responding to the recommendations of your committee, you will find enthusiastic support and encouragement. The committee's patience with your progress may be short-lived if you absent yourself for extended time periods and/or repeatedly offer excuses for not progressing. Students with significant personal crises reported that by attending to their dissertations, they were able to see progress in at least this aspect of their lives. Try to get done with your dissertation as rapidly as possible.

Your meetings with your committee are academic conversations, talking about ideas and processes. Be ready to explain your thinking based on your interpretation of published materials and expect to listen to other perspectives. Ultimately, it is important that you provide expansive explanations of the decisions you made in each aspect of your study, while listening to and considering alternative viewpoints. Your opinion should derive from a comprehensive understanding of the literature and the historical evolution of your academic discipline. Refer to specific sources in your explanations. Your progress from a doctoral student to a student "ready for orals" will be marked by your growing proficiencies in these types of interaction.

Learning What to Expect from your Chair and Readers

There are several ways to find out your committee's expectations. For example:

- Ask each committee member.
- Ask students who are currently working with one or more of the professors on your committee.
- Review dissertations completed during the past five years with one or more of the professors on your committee.

You are encouraged to obtain multiple responses. By accessing several perspectives you increase the quantity of ideas to consider while potentially corroborating the information, insights, and perspectives from these different sources.

There are questions which you might prepare to pose to your potential dissertation chair and readers. These are organized into two groups: initial, general questions, and those with a more specific focus, addressing issues which evolve once you've started working together.

Initial, general questions for the committee

- How do you usually work with your doctoral students?
- What do you think are my responsibilities?
- In what ways can I expect that you will help me?
- Will you give me assignments each week?
- Are there other students who are working with you on a similar topic, whom I might work with?
- Do you have a research group that meets periodically to talk about projects?
- Do you have preferences for one research methodology, one theory, or one topic over others? Why do you prefer these?
- Is there a way in which I might work on one of your research projects for my dissertation?
- Will we be able to meet during the summer and during semester breaks?
- Will you meet with me if I have nothing written?
- How will I get feedback?
- What progress do I need to make each semester?
- What happens if I don't finish in two years?
- How do I know if I am making good progress?

Continued on next page

- Can you provide me with guidelines for how long this will take based on your experiences with other doctoral students?
- Can we establish a schedule to organize my work?
- Who has to evaluate my work?
- What are the characteristics of an acceptable dissertation proposal?
- What problems can I expect to encounter?

The more information you have at the outset, the more you can prepare for your responsibilities, and the less likely it is that you will encounter conflicts between your expectations and reality. Once you've started working, there are additional questions you may want to pose.

Specific questions for your committee

- What do you think I should do next?
- Do I need to summarize in writing all that I have done during the time between our meetings?
- When do I actually start writing my dissertation?
- Where might I find dissertation proposals to read?
- Where might I find dissertations to read?
- Which dissertations do you think would be useful for me to read? What should I particularly look for in these dissertations?
- Is there a predetermined, specific format that I need to use when I write my proposal or my dissertation? Where do I find out what that is? How will you help me to learn and follow this format?
- How "polished" must the text be that I give you to read?
- May I leave materials for you to read in your office mail box?
- Should I e-mail you whenever I have a question?
- What are acceptable times to phone you? (Get all available phone numbers and beepers, if offered.)
- How frequently can I expect to get feedback?

Keep your committee informed of your activities. Let them know if your life is changing in ways which may impact on your dissertation writing; for example, perhaps you need to take on another job for financial reasons, you are looking for a new position, or you are getting married. Professors like to know that you are a serious student, cognizant of your commitment to doing your dissertation. If you absent yourself from the academic community without explaining your new pressures, they may take you and your work less seriously, and neglect to mention texts or conferences which may be useful to you, or to encourage you to finish.

While you are informing your committee of changes in your priorities, they, too, might be experiencing major events in their lives. You may find that changes need to be made in your committee due to death or illness, for example. These always complicate and lengthen the process. At times the student needs to start all over again, with a totally new focus. The more rapidly you progress, the less likely these changes will occur.

Expect at least one crisis. For each student the crisis will be different, and for each it will be generated from a different source. But expect that there will be at least one curve ball at some time. The unexpected event might come in the decision of one of your readers to relocate. It might be that there is a fire in your office where you keep all of your dissertation materials. It might be that the dissertation proposal which your committee accepts gets questioned by some other approving group. It might be that the people who agreed to serve as your "subjects" or participants have a change of heart. It might be that your spouse decides to end your marriage. It is unlikely that all of these things will happen to any one person, but all of these have happened to people and most have continued to complete their degrees. They persevered tenaciously. It will not be easy. You can only be assured that it will be memorable! And almost to a person, doctoral recipients are happy that they endured the process.

Working with Your Committee

As you work with your committee, you will become increasingly responsible for making decisions. Initially the faculty will guide you, offering advice about the form and content of each part of the dissertation proposal and dissertation. They will expect you to follow this advice, as well as take on responsibility for exploring resources beyond what they suggest. You need to keep them posted on your journey, explaining how your thinking about your topic is evolving, what sources are contributing to this development, and what new questions are emerging. The entire research process results in an increasing number of questions, a new sense of complexities and new insights.

The balance of responsibility and of knowledge gradually changes during the time when you are working on your dissertation as presented graphically in Figure 7.1. Although the faculty will provide general guidelines, you will craft a unique proposal which responds to the specific research question you have chosen and which draws on your unique strengths and experiences.

When you meet with faculty, they are likely to engage in conversations about your work, helping you to think more deeply about your topic, offering you a forum for trying out some of the new language which you are learning, while you are informing them of your progress. In your conversations they will help you to identify gaps and inconsistencies in your thinking, an essential element in promoting your work. These conversations are probably valued as much by the faculty as by the student since faculty typically seek opportunities for scholarly talk. You can expect that your committee is likely to pose numerous questions. Typical questions are listed in the box below. You might find it useful to consider your answers to these questions as you are writing and revising your proposal.

Use this time to practice expansive explanations of your thinking while evaluating your consistency and your depth of understanding. When noting weaknesses, you will want to enrich your knowledge in advance of your committee's identification of a gap in your knowledge. While it is impossible for anyone to know "everything," there are key issues which you should be able

---

Questions faculty are likely to ask you

- Why do you want to do this research?
- How did you pick this topic?
- How are you doing with your literature search?
- What are your hunches about what your findings may reveal?
- What are your reasons for choosing this strategy?
- How is your study likely to contribute to our knowledge?
- What other procedures might you consider?
- What are the competing theories which are being addressed in your study?
- What is the basic "argument" which you are addressing in your study? How well are you addressing this issue?
- What are you going to do next and why?
- What problems are you finding? How are you handling them?
- What criteria will you use in selecting your sample?
- What theories (implicitly or explicitly) are contributing to the design of your study?
- Can you document the historical evolution of this theory?
- What confidence do you have that your analysis is comprehensive?
- How will the findings of your study influence our knowledge and/or practice?

---

to explain. You also should be able to say that you do not know and that you will research the issue. Any area of ignorance relevant to your study should be addressed in the process of doing your dissertation.

Expect these conversations with your professors to be opportunities for you to learn from them while you demonstrate your expanding understanding of the discipline and of your specific research focus. These interactions are a prelude to the formal conversation which will occur at your oral examination or oral defense.

The Complexities of the Committee's Power

The faculty are the ones who typically initiate the necessary approvals for your proposal and eventually for your dissertation. This imbalance of power prevails throughout the process. And inequalities in power are played out in different ways with each person having a unique experience. Relationships between students and faculty are complicated. There are numerous reasons for this:

- The university establishes a hierarchical structure with the faculty having the authority (read that as power) to recommend students for graduation, for example. Thus, students are dependent on faculty in this relationship.
- Ultimately, the students in a doctoral program become colleagues of the faculty, frequently teaching on the staff of the university or other local institutions. Some faculty resist this transition. They believe that "once a student, always a student." For others, this is an important phase which they consciously and overtly support, seeking to participate in the apprenticeship of their future colleagues.
- Some professors establish a "tough love" stance wherein they believe their responsibility is to help the student, but the student must both ask for help and show that she or he has independently worked at trying to resolve the issue.
- Some professors prefer to have as little as possible to do with the daily development of the dissertation, seeing it only when the student is convinced she or he has finished with it. Others want to hear frequent updates on progress and to participate, for example, in the data analysis process.

The committee's intent and concerns at times are perceived as abusive. There are numerous contexts in which their influence is felt. Harvard University was catapulted into the limelight recently when one of their doctoral students committed suicide. In a letter left for his advisor, Jason Altom referred to his advisor's comment that his project had "no intellectual contribution" (Schneider, 1998, p. A12). Schneider, a reporter, noted:

> More than most students ... Mr. Altom feared and revered his adviser. ... "People have a perception that Corey [the advisor] can make or break your career." That fear is not unfounded. ... Good jobs, prestigious grants, even tenure depend on strong letters of recommendation. ... As an aftermath to this student's suicide, the department has established a new plan intended to avoid the problem of isolation and of control over a student's future.
>
> (Schneider, 1998, pp. A12–14)

The faculty's power is clearly a concern in the academic world. In an article in the *Chronicle of Higher Education*, Leatherman (1997) notes the University of Pennsylvania "has a strict rule of thumb: 'you do not ask your students to work for you on activities that serve you personally but are not affiliated with academic work'" (p. A11). There is an additional admonition from Elizabeth Fox-Genovese who notes that the employment of graduate students by professors is "an extremely complicated relationship, and there are good reasons to avoid it" (p. A11).

A related matter involves publishing student work. Some professors will only mentor on the condition that the student writes an article on the dissertation with the professor's name listed as first author. Some students look on this as advantageous, jump-starting their publishing record, acknowledging the fact that their professor's name on the article is likely to bring more acclaim than their own. Some faculty consider this "the least" that the student can do to reciprocate for all the time they will devote to the project. Other faculty are appalled at this tradition.

In some rare cases, students have a sense that faculty have actually appropriated their work without giving credit to the student for doing the work. According to the *New York Times* of September 24, 1997, "they seldom take legal action because they fear jeopardizing their degree or their references" (p. A25). While these occurrences are rare, they do happen. You need to prepare to deal with these situations if you are confronted with such dilemmas. Institutions create bureaucratic procedures for addressing issues such as harassment. You should become aware of the policies that prevail at your university. They are likely to be published in handbooks and in *Bulletins* as well as being posted conspicuously on university bulletin boards. In case there are no such precautions available bureaucratically within the university, you may find support in your affiliations with students and other faculty. The informal networks you create may guard you against these potential dilemmas while providing essential support and guidance when needed.

Notes

1 Changes in committees may occur when faculty take sabbatical leave, leave the university, retire from the university, move to another geographic area, become incapacitated, or die. Frequently committee members remain in place, regardless of their changed status with the university, but sometimes this is not possible. Whenever there are changes in a committee, there is a chance that there will be a change in the expectations of the members, or a change in the enthusiasm and support for your project. These changes have been known to cause students to have to start all over again, getting a new topic and a new committee. This is particularly true if there is a change in the chair.

Since you cannot predict these eventualities, you need to do all in your power to try to avoid these events. Working rapidly is one strategy. Try to have "all your ducks in order" so that once you start working on your dissertation you will be able to devote significant energy to completing it in a brief time period. Also, try to monitor what is happening in your committee's lives so that you are not surprised by the changes. An additional strategy is to keep up your positive relationships with all the faculty in your program so that if you need to substitute one faculty for another, you will not be "iced out."

2 The dissertation proposal is a contract between you and the university to accomplish one project. Depending on the specificity required in your dissertation, you may have some "wiggle room," but usually the dissertation proposal identifies a very specific focus which must be consistent with your dissertation. An alternative strategy is to modify the dissertation proposal as your dissertation evolves, and then seek approval for the modified proposal prior to seeking approval of the dissertation. Most institutions are still working from a hypothesis-testing perspective where more definitive proposals are appropriate. As hypothesis-generating and ethnographic proposals are developed, more open-ended expectations will prevail, reducing the need to modify a proposal.

8 Creating a Professional Setting
Student-colleagues and Other Important Resources

> It was a challenging, but pleasant experience. I worked hard, but received support in my efforts. This was a good experience for me.

> Every stage of development was memorable. I will never be the person I was prior to the completion of my dissertation. I have been incredibly enriched by the process.

While your dissertation committee is crucial to your success, you are wise to expand your community of potential advisors and supporters. This additional group may provide strategies to help you work effectively with your committee, and offer alternative perspectives on your experiences with your committee and your research. By intentionally seeking to expand your community, you are prepared to deal with a variety of problems likely to present themselves while writing your dissertation.

As a developing researcher, you are becoming expert at posing questions to acquire the information you need. Now you need to use this developing expertise to your personal benefit, comparing responses from multiple, independent sources. In this process you reduce the likelihood of operating on misinformation. You will need to decide where to get the best advice on a particular topic. Some people may send you down the wrong path intentionally or by chance. Be vigilant in checking all the information you receive.

While doctoral students frequently feel isolated as they pursue their degrees, this is neither a useful nor necessarily an accurate stance. There are many people who have the potential to promote your progress. We will consider the important roles which are frequently played by student-colleagues, denizens of the university community, and colleagues at professional conferences.

Student-colleagues

Some doctoral students identify colleague support as crucial in completing their degrees. Students offer each other emotional and academic support, both of which are important in pursuing your degree. One reason students reach out to other students is that they feel comfortable talking with peers. A second reason is their similar status in the university. Students have different perspectives on the whole enterprise from faculty. Students rely on each other for important information. For example:

- They explain the details which somehow seem to escape the attention of the faculty.
- They help to figure out what is expected at different points in the process.
- They share your tension when you are waiting to get a professor's feedback.
- They share their information about what happens at doctoral orals.
- They suggest some strategies for dealing with professors.
- They explain how they went about writing their "literature review."
- They tell you where to get useful university documents detailing the dissertation process.
- They help to pick up the pieces after your work has been criticized in front of your peers.
- They help you identify potential faculty when forming your committee.
- They review their steps in identifying their research topic.
- They share their progress with you, helping you to learn from their experiences.
- They take time to celebrate with you when you have reached an important stage.
- They keep you focused when you become discouraged.
- They work with you in collecting and/or analyzing your data.
- They suggest how your ideas can be presented more clearly.
- They proofread your text.
- They figure out which APA citation format to use.
- They guard your materials in the library.
- They tell you when a new publication has arrived.
- They alert you to an article which may bear on your topic.
- They celebrate your hard work.
- They seek your advice, learning from your experiences.
- They tell you when your dissertation chair is sitting in the booth behind you.
- They commiserate with you when you feel depressed.

And the list could go on.

The point is that the student network is a very valuable resource for all doctoral students. Students know information that no one else does. It is to your advantage to connect with other students, to have access to this multifaceted, knowledgeable, and sympathetic support system.

Small groups of doctoral students support each other's progress and learn together. If the group includes people at different stages in the dissertation process, neophytes learn from those who have succeeded while the more experienced become conscious of the "method in the madness" in their explanations to beginners. Gilles identifies the need for multiple support groups in "Everybody needs a 'grip,'" suggesting that:

> Doctoral students need a variety of groups, from formal seminars to informal lunch groups. ... Three sources of support are necessary and vital: an adviser who makes you stretch, a group of faculty and students who discuss research and challenge one another, and an informal group that can solve an individual's particular problem through their shared candor, insightfulness, irreverence, humor, or any combination. The writing of the dissertation isn't a time for being alone and writing in a closed room; it should be a time to nurture, invest in, and benefit from the collegial friendships begun in course work that will continue throughout our professional careers.
>
> (Gilles, 1996, p. 52)

There is another compelling reason for advancing the need to seek out colleagues. Part of your goal in getting the degree is to enter a new community. Now is the time to start building that community.

You cannot do this alone. You will need to allow yourself to say that you "don't know," and along with that, you need to find ways to become more knowledgeable. The companionship of others struggling with similar concerns is mutually supportive. And the struggles which you survive today will become the core of the humorous lore you repeat as your group progresses professionally.

Your experiences working with colleagues on your dissertation will carry over into other professional activities. Our professional work is frequently the product of collaboration: setting up a conference program, searching for new faculty, planning a research project, and evaluating programs. The people you worked with on your dissertation can become an important resource in your professional life-after-dissertation if you learn to work well when you are students together.

Frequently your student-colleagues are the only ones who truly understand what you are going through. They know all of the professors and their idiosyncrasies. They can sympathize with you when you are down; they will take the time to help you to see the light at the end of the tunnel, and keep you on track.

In addition to the emotional support offered by your peers, there is academic support as well. You promote each other's learning through talking about what you are doing. Your professional conversations offer you a comfortable setting for trying out the new technical language and ideas which predominate in your readings. Your small informal group(s) serve to bridge your two worlds, helping you to become more comfortable with the specialized language of your profession while conversing with supportive neophytes. Student-colleagues are also an excellent source of information as you search for potential committee members.

Some useful questions students pose to each other include:

- How do/did you work with Professor X?
- What are/were some good ways to get done?

- What problems can I expect to encounter?
- What strategies are useful for me to adopt?
- How often did you get to talk with Professor X? Was that frequent enough?
- Did Professor X keep appointments?
- Did you need to confirm all appointments?
- Were the appointments at times which were convenient for *you*?
- Were there distractions during your appointment time?
- Does Professor X give useful comments to advance your work?
- Is Professor X supportive – or do you feel foolish with him or her?
- Did you feel that you were treated differently from other students?
- Did you feel that you needed to do work for Professor X (xeroxing, baby sitting, or driving to the airport, etc.) in exchange for Professor X's help?
- Did you teach, conduct research, and grade papers as part of your training or in exchange for assistance on your dissertation?
- Did you have to agree to publish your dissertation with Professor X?
- Which professors get along?
- What problems might I expect?
- How do/did you negotiate problems?

Some students isolate themselves, believing groups are distractions. Without these diversions, they believe they will finish more rapidly. They frequently regret this decision, and eventually seek ways to become incorporated into groups. Isolating yourself from the dissertation community leaves you vulnerable to being forgotten by your peers and your program faculty. Those students who get "lost," either literally or figuratively, are most likely to drop out. Ultimately, the issue is not to isolate yourself, nor allow yourself to be isolated from students or faculty.

So what can you do? You can find on-going groups of students who will allow you to join with them, or you can start a group. Usually some activity in your program brings everyone together, such as the courses, candidacy experience, or dissertation seminar. Students who form study groups benefit academically and emotionally, meeting informally with these colleagues on a continuing basis.

The University Community

There are a wide variety of people who comprise your university community beyond your committee and your student-colleagues. All can potentially support your progress. We will consider a few such opportunities.

Libraries

Many contemporary researchers are doing virtually all of their library research on computer terminals, perhaps miles from the place where these materials are housed. While on the one hand I can admire the expertise, I am fearful of the possibility that when you are surfing the net, you may forgo the serendipitous experiences that occur when browsing in the library.

Wandering among the stacks, we meet interesting people and we also spot titles worthy of investigation – names which we've heard before but whose connection with our own work we are not sure about and attractively bound works which please our aesthetic senses. These accidental sightings may lead to uncharted, exciting discoveries. It is advantageous to find bridges between disciplines, noting overlap in some important realms, as a way to see the world through new lenses – all part of the research process. When you look at articles in journals, look at the whole journal. In addition to reading the article which was your initial goal, review the table of contents, other articles in that issue, perhaps some book reviews, and certainly the book advertisements and conference announcements. You need truly to immerse yourself in your professional community, and journals are one easy resource which invite your participation.

You will also find a valuable resource in a friendly librarian. Not only will you get assistance in finding materials technologically, but you will also get access to texts which may enable you to connect important disciplines, events, or luminaries in your field. Librarians can also expedite your request for inter-library loans, for computer searches, and for new library acquisitions. These "information specialists" can facilitate your access to materials that draw on their expertise. They can alert you to times when the library will be closed or noisy construction work is scheduled. They also can tell you when a publication which seems related to your research has arrived, or when they've come across a new source of information which may be of interest to you.

As you wander in the library you will also meet compatriots, people who are similarly engaged in research. You may strike up conversations with people reading from the same journals as you are, becoming aware that although they are affiliated with a different university department, they have similar academic concerns. The opportunity for expanding your understanding of your "discipline" and other, related disciplines may present itself in this context. The university community is diverse in many ways, with some core values which resonate across department boundaries. Your engagement in library research may promote your understanding of that culture.

Computer Technicians

The computer technicians are a crucial resource. Not only can they get you up and running on current technology, they can apprise you of new software and new equipment which might facilitate your work. In addition, you may succeed in convincing them to order some hardware or software which might assist you.

If you use the computer facility on a regular basis, you will probably find a space which is most comfortable for you. If you are friendly, you may find that space "reserved" for you. On the other hand, you may find that your equipment is frequently "down" or your software has been removed from the system. By being friendly to all, you will not only feel better about yourself, but you are likely to make more rapid progress.

University Security

The security personnel in your school see *everything*. They see you come and go. They know who your friends are and when you are glum. If you are friendly to them, they may even become important supports: cheering you up when you are down, telling your friends where to find you, and securing materials you inadvertently leave behind. They will greet you after a holiday break, and celebrate your progress in your program. If you let them into your world, they somehow understand that what you are doing is not easy, and they are happy for you as you move closer to your degree.

Personnel in Local Shops

The book store personnel can help you in many ways. For example, they may locate books which are in your field, expand their list of offerings in your field, expedite your request for materials, and tell you of recent releases which are in areas of potential interest to you. The coffee-bar workers will allow you to sit for hours, cleaning up your mess, and maintaining a comfortable climate, perhaps even engaging in conversation with you about your work. Their questions may require you to explain your ideas carefully and expansively. When you switch from the specialized language in your professional journals you think more clearly about what precisely you are studying and how it may be important to life in general. Although financially they may be disappointed to see you graduate, they will celebrate with you, and feel proud of their contribution to your progress.

Professional Conferences and Colleagues

A number of national and local professional conferences have encouraged doctoral students in a variety of ways. Seek these out, soliciting recommendations from your committee. The journals, which publish articles in your discipline are typically connected with professional organizations which sponsor conferences. The journals also carry advertisements of professional and university-based conferences. When you join professional organizations your name is placed on mailing lists to receive notices of conferences. You may also find it useful to contact professors and students at other universities who are working "in your field," and to inquire from them about upcoming professional conferences. Conferences are particularly useful for a number of reasons:

•   Most of the people who attend these sessions seem to be supportive, finding ways to help others.

- These are annual, predictable settings where you can (if you wish) be almost anonymous, listening to what others are going through, and learning vicariously.
- Experts in the field who attend these sessions have been both insightful and supportive, helping students in a variety of ways including such issues as:
  - getting along with their professors;
  - finding an appropriate site to do their study;
  - seeking ways to analyze their data;
  - seeking ways to understand what they have found; and
  - offering pre-publication copies of texts.

- In this community the participants frequently follow up with each other, asking how things are going after the conference ends. They also renew acquaintances annually, recount major events during the year, and mark their progress toward completion.
- The settings are generally small, with groups of fifteen to thirty people engaging in these activities. (Although there might be hundreds if not thousands of people at the whole conference, there are sessions specifically focused for doctoral students which are more humane in scope, encouraging the opportunity for all to participate in the conversation.)

You need not be a member of these organizations to attend their meetings. Most offer student membership with significantly reduced fees. This membership usually includes numerous publications and other mailings, for example at least one journal, newsletters, announcements about conferences, and calls for proposals to present at conferences. The networks which are created at these events are noteworthy, lasting years, and stretching across oceans. Some useful professional conferences are noted below.

American Educational Research Association (AERA)

(1230 17th Street, NW, Washington, DC 20036, USA; http://www.aera.net)
AERA has an annual conference, typically held in March or April, which brings together thousands of researchers worldwide. There are some special sessions where doctoral students are particularly nurtured. Some of these are sponsored by the separate divisions within the organization. AERA has a Special Interest Group (SIG) that focuses exclusively on doctoral students. The group's business meeting and newsletter are intended to provide guidance for doctoral students in completing their degrees. AERA has a number of publications which are likely to be useful to you in your research including: *Educational Researcher* (*ER*), *American Educational Research Journal* (*AERJ*), and *Review of Educational Research* (*RER*).

University of Pennsylvania Ethnography Conference

(Center for Urban Ethnography, Graduate School of Education, University of Pennsylvania, 3700 Walnut Street, Philadelphia, PA 19104, USA; http://www.gse.upenn.edu/cue)

The University of Pennsylvania convenes an annual conference on ethnography which usually takes place in February or March. At this time in addition to formal plenary sessions, the doctoral students and experienced researchers present "works in progress" and inquiries about data analysis. The sessions are led by respected researchers who, along with the assembled participants, provide useful and friendly feedback. At lunch, in between sessions, at dinner and breakfast, conversations started during sessions are continued. A book of "Abstracts" of paper presentations is published along with this event.

National Council of Teachers of English (NCTE)

(1111 West Kenyon Road, Urbana, IL 61801 USA; http://www.ncte.org)

There are three activities sponsored by NCTE which are particularly focused on doctoral students.

- At the annual conference (usually held in November), the Doctoral Assembly meets. This is a small group of students from universities across the nation who are typically working on dissertations addressing issues of language, literacy, and/or learning. The group consists mainly of doctoral students, but there is usually at least one person with degree in hand who offers additional information and alternative perspectives not typically available to the students. There is a newsletter which is sponsored by this group. Their informal gatherings enable participants to share general concerns while also creating the opportunity for small group talk about precise research issues. They also network about job prospects at this meeting. Membership of the Doctoral Assembly is approximately $10 per year.
- At the NCTE Spring Conference (usually held in March or April), the Ramon Veal Seminar is an all-day conference within a conference. In advance of the seminar, current doctoral students as well as doctoral advisors and current researchers submit brief statements about their research and the issues they would like the group to help them address. There is no separate membership in the Ramon Veal Seminar. Participants do, however, pay for the cost of duplicating the packet of materials delivered in advance of the conference, frequently returning on an annual basis, attending from early on in their doctoral studies and continuing after completing the dissertation. Membership of the NCTE is available with reduced rates for students. Publications include *Research in the Teaching of English* (*RTE*), *English Education* (*EE*), *College Composition and Communication* (*CCC*), *Language Arts* (*LA*), *English Journal* (*EJ*), and *College English* (*CE*).

Creating a professional setting

- The annual weekend conference in February sponsored by the Research Assembly limits attendance to approximately 150 participants who offer presentations and small group discussions of research projects and processes. In addition to several presentations by well-known researchers, there is also the opportunity for doctoral students to get advice from other doctoral students and experienced researchers at this event.

Teacher researcher/teacher conversation groups

Growing numbers of experienced teachers are creating "grass roots" groups discussing research. These groups are another useful resource since all participants are working on developing research projects, going through the same academic procedures as doctoral students go through in their dissertation research. Many of these groups are affiliated with local National Writing Project sites. Others are independent, initiated by a group of like-minded professionals who meet in each other's homes and work towards contributing to the school reform conversations. Many of these have established web sites, making it convenient for researchers to communicate frequently. Addresses are listed below for your convenience:

AERA Special Interest Group – Teacher as Researcher
c/o American Educational Research Association
1230 17th Street, NW, Washington, DC 20036, USA

International Conference on Teacher Research
Bishop's University, School of Education
Lennoxville, Quebec, Canada J1M 1V7

Re-Thinking Schools
1001 East Keefe Avenue
Milwaukee, WI 53212, USA
Rethink@execpc.com

There are many opportunities for doctoral students to reach out to others for emotional and academic support. Informal networks are sometimes more influential than the formal ones established at universities. Along with providing additional perspectives, doctoral students travel to conferences, preparing for professional lives as conference attendees and presenters while increasing their familiarity with life in other cities. When you look beyond your dissertation committee, you will discover a rich and enthusiastic mix of new colleagues to meet worldwide.

By drawing on the combined expertise of your dissertation committee along with student-colleagues, other university resources, colleagues at professional conferences, and on e-mail, you will have access to a broad range of perspectives which will facilitate the completion of your doctoral dissertation. You will also have the support of professional colleagues, which you may reciprocate. There is a large community of researchers to join. Welcome! Enjoy it!

9 Developing a Productive Setting

I learned to trust my instincts – to trust my ability to infer what is behind a person's words, actions, or at least my ability to propose a few possibilities for explaining their words, actions, etc.

As I wrote my dissertation, I learned to appreciate the questioner within myself. It helped me move beyond the obvious and to work through the blocks as I investigated and analyzed my data. I also saw how important my goal-setting skills are when I want to complete something. I learned to have a thicker skin when receiving advice from a mentor. I learned to look beyond the logical for anomalies and patterns. I learned pacing and I learned to write succinctly so that the message is clear and powerful to the reader. Most importantly, I learned I am a writer.

As a doctoral student, you need consciously to create supportive settings which will contribute to your success. Your own mind-set, along with those of your family and colleagues at work, contributes significantly to your success. Fortunate students find themselves in a community of academically oriented folk, celebrated for their willingness to take on the challenges and the responsibilities of a doctoral program.

Part-time students, in particular, are surprised when their announced decision to pursue a doctoral degree is met with little enthusiasm by their friends, colleagues, and family. There may be many reasons for this phenomenon, such as jealousy, competition, and mystification. People at home or at work may be envious of your ambition. They may wish they had qualities which they ascribe to those who enroll in doctoral programs: intelligence, energy, confidence, time, and money. They may believe you are being selfish. Most frequently, with no idea what it means to be in a doctoral program, they may be reluctant to admit their lack of understanding, and instead convey an attitude of not caring.

People look on you differently when you become a doctoral student. This is as true at your workplace as at home. Some consider your being in a doctoral program a wonderful accomplishment; for others it is a threat. Find the ones who will support you. Protect yourself from the others.

If few people in your everyday life are enthusiastic about your decision, you need to accept this fact and find settings which offer support, while acknowledging the possibility that you might need to go the road alone. If you are dependent on the emotional and/or financial support of others, you will need to attend to this immediately. Some options include:

- finding a way to garner support with at least one friend;
- resolving to be strong and independent; or
- changing your mind, at least temporarily, until you can obtain the support you require.

There are a multitude of settings where you can find support. We will focus on you, your family, and your job, starting with you in your role as doctoral student.

The Doctoral Student's Mind-set

Because the writing of a dissertation takes so much time, and because it inevitably changes the ways and/or times in which you interact with friends, colleagues, and relatives, a clear decision to commit to the writing of the dissertation is essential. The first crucial ingredient in your success is being personally committed to completing your dissertation. This commitment may take several forms. You may feel a "personal attachment ... towards the project," or have a "personal belief in myself – that what I'm doing is important and good and of value to myself and others," or you might find that others are "valuing my ideas" or that you have a "passionate desire to know the answer to a research question."[1]

An additional element in the decision is that it will be "worth it." Those who have gone through the process warn: "Don't write a thesis unless you're absolutely sure that you're ready for the sacrifice it involves;" "It totally takes over your life and interferes with all your choices;" I did not realize "how physically and mentally exhausting it is." A doctoral student must have a strong positive response to the inquiry "Do I really want it?" In the mind of each doctoral student, the benefits have to exceed the drawbacks.

Having a personal commitment, a will to succeed, is necessary, but not sufficient. You will also need the strength to endure the many potential difficulties you will encounter as you progress in writing your dissertation. Along with your personal resolve, you will need effective organization skills, sufficient financial resources, time, and an intellectual inquisitiveness.

Some Essential Qualities

Being a self-starter and having self-discipline are crucial characteristics of doctoral graduates. After succeeding in courses and examinations at institutionally established times, the doctoral student is required to become virtually an independent learner. Dissertation writing is consistently experienced as an isolating activity. Each person progresses at a different rate, studying a different topic, and collaborating with a different doctoral committee. Each student has the responsibility for scheduling independent meetings during professors' office hours.

Concurrent with inventorying your personal qualities, resolve to minimize changes in your life which may influence the progress you make on your dissertation. For example, defer moving to a new geographic setting or accepting more demanding responsibilities at work, to enable you to dedicate your energies to accomplishing this one project. Frequently, students have difficulty in saying "No" to new work opportunities. When this happens, usually the dissertation gets placed on the back-burner while major energy is invested in a new project.

Your dissertation will only get written when you make it your number one priority, deferring activities to after you have completed your dissertation. But, you need not become a hermit. Successful doctoral students find ways to balance their dissertation work with other activities. They hop between and among many worlds, but always keep the writing of the dissertation as paramount in their minds, as apparent in their allocation of time.

Effective management and organizational skills are essential. Doctoral students and faculty highlighted five essential characteristics of successful students. These are listed below and presented graphically in Figure 9.1.

- Be *goal-directed*.
- *Organize your time* to meet your goal.
- Assure your *financial resources* to meet your goal.
- Establish a *scholarly attitude* to continuing your learning in the process of meeting your goal.
- Create a *supportive setting* to facilitate your achieving your goal.

These points offer specific advice which may be useful for your own strategizing.

Be goal-directed

Know what you want to accomplish. You may choose a pragmatic approach, determining to write an "acceptable dissertation," or you may choose a more demanding one, aiming to accomplish at least two objectives simultaneously. You may see your dissertation as an opportunity to make a significant contribution to your field, and/or you may view your dissertation as a vehicle which will move your career along, providing a credential with expertise in a particular field. It is important to know what *you* want to accomplish as you establish the support system essential to achieving your goal. Be sure to keep your goals realistic; start small, if necessary. Don't set yourself up for failure.

Being goal-directed, you are tenacious, dedicated to accomplishing your dream. Keep on working until your dream is achieved. Self-discipline is essential. If you make a commitment to yourself to work on your dissertation every morning from 5 to 7 am, fulfill your promise. "Personal circumstances impede commitment and continuity of effort," is a frequent observation of doctoral

Figure 9.1   *The doctoral student's ideal world*

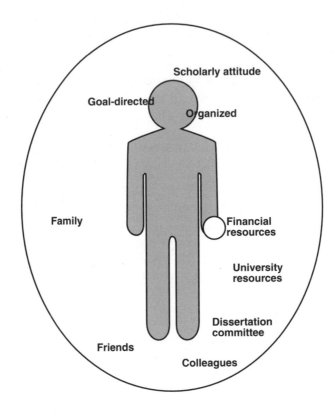

students. (The phrasing of this quotation is potentially significant. It might reflect the doctoral student's passive role. Alternatively it might provide evidence of the effect of being instructed to avoid the use of "I." Clearly that style pervades many of the responses offered in this study.)

You need to be firmly committed to getting your degree, or you will not have the stamina to resist all the distractions which are likely to divert your progress. You need to find an inner strength that you will not get from others.

Organize your time to meet your goal

Create a system for organizing your work on this large-scale project. Work on parts which contribute to the whole. For example, work on one chapter, or even one part of a chapter at a time. Divide and conquer! Be able to identify your achievement of sub-goals along the way. Knowing the stages in the process, you can mark your progress on a checklist which you create. (See Appendix E for a sample checklist.)

Establish a consistent block of time to work every day, undisturbed by other responsibilities, time when your exclusive task is to work on your dissertation. The more time you devote to your dissertation, the sooner you are likely to get done. Note this schedule in your appointment book, making this time inaccessible for other activities.

Identify your own realistic yet demanding deadlines revising these as you proceed. Expect to invest as much as six years of your life in this process. (The length of time will vary among programs and among individual participants. Clearly part-time, commuter students are likely to take longer than full-time, residential students, and students conducting hypothesis-testing studies are likely to get done sooner than those doing hypothesis-generating studies.) Even though coursework can be completed quickly, you will need time to navigate the system and to write your dissertation. Students find that once they focus *all* of their energies on the dissertation (when getting done becomes an obsession), they finish fairly quickly. Although your dissertation may be the most important activity at this moment in your life, it probably is not that important for many others. "*You* need to take control of the process and the pacing."

> If you cannot take control of your time, you will never finish. Do not clean house. If necessary, do not let your mother or other critical housewife-types visit until you are finished. And then, let them take you out to dinner. Teach all family members routine housekeeping chores. It will build their character although they won't realize this at first.

Assure your financial resources to meet your goal

The possibility of "exhausting financial resources" before your completion can be a daunting experience. Get a realistic projection of the amount of money you are likely to spend in the process of completing your degree by asking current and graduating students. Include expenses for transportation, books, xeroxing, typing, and tuition. When working with restricted finances, you might consider some options. Are there ways to defer some expenses to the future when I may have a new job and perhaps an increased salary? Are there some expenses I can avoid by using the library's resources more extensively? Are there some things which I would like to have, but do not need at this moment? Inquire about scholarships, fellowships, assistantships, loans, and part-time employment opportunities at the university. Share your concerns with your dissertation committee. They may be able to direct you to some financial resources.

Establish a scholarly attitude of continued learning in the process of meeting your goal

Expect to continue to learn in the process of writing your dissertation. Your dissertation is not a final examination. It is a new learning experience, an apprenticeship in research. This is the time to increase your understandings about conducting research, about knowledge in your discipline, and about how to write a research report. Learning is what students and scholars do. Students frequently believe that the dissertation is an exercise to prove that they have learned the content of their courses. Faculty frequently believe the dissertation is an activity to promote the acquisition and development of more sophisticated scholarly skills and knowledge. Clearly with these different perspectives, conflict and tension are inevitable. The attentive student resolves these problems rapidly.

Currently the aims to be achieved by writing a dissertation are being discussed (for e.g., see Olson and Drew, 1998). From a historical perspective, the dissertation was initially viewed as the first scholarly publication. This goal has been modified in many settings. The university program you enrolled in probably has a tradition which you may either challenge or continue. (If you challenge it, expect repercussions! The purpose of this book is to guide you to complete your dissertation. Once you have accomplished this goal, you may be in the vanguard of those seeking to revise this entire process. Clearly a critique of the current procedures is needed and will be forthcoming.)

Expect to become frustrated and resolve to be resourceful in finding ways to deal with these tensions. Expect to develop independence as a learner, making such decisions as:

- What's important?
- When do I stop collecting data?
- What is my role in the community where I do my research?
- When is a good time to stop reading and start writing?

Articulating your confusion and need for knowledge is the first step towards getting answers to your questions.

Believe in yourself and your own capabilities. If you've succeeded academically this far, you must have what you need to go further. Avoid the syndrome of thinking you're supposed to know everything, as reflected in this student's testimony:

> I had little to no idea how to use the materials in the archives to which I had access. The ... Library seemed to be full of scholars who already knew what they were doing and why. There were no institutional processes for learning how to use the resources. Asking questions seemed to mark me as inadequate and amateur rather than curious and enthusiastic.

Another remarked: "I was reluctant to reveal my personal concerns. I thought it might potentially damage my future, my completion, my employment, my advancement, my publications, my conference invitations, and opportunities for grants, and awards." These are self-destructive stances.

You need to find a way to access information. One way to do this is to believe in your ability to discover answers to your questions. Expect learning to take time. Be patient with yourself and *persevere*. In addition, ask your supportive colleagues.

Create a supportive setting to facilitate achieving your goal

Comments about isolation are common in doctoral students' experiences:

> I thought it would be a collaborative experience, but instead, it was a very lonely, isolating one.

> Being away from my family and friends and doing things totally alone was very difficult.

> I did not understand the remoteness of my friends, colleagues, and professors.

> I was surprised how little support existed outside of the mentor.

> When I accepted the fact that I was alone in this effort, I researched my methodology by identifying experts, reading their books, and *talking with them on the phone*. I was very pleased with the responses. They answered their phones personally, were very receptive to my inquiries, and spent as much time with me as most of my committee.

The isolation comes as a surprise. Resourceful doctoral students create a supportive community where they celebrate each other's progress, profit from each other's experiences, keep each other on task, and critique drafts, all in the process of assisting each other in meeting goals.

As in your doctoral research, where you will seek multiple data sources to inform your response to your research question, seek multiple sources for your personal support, but always remember that *you* must be your strongest advocate. The degree is for you, and others do not have the same vested interest as you. Regardless of how many people are potentially available to work with you, ultimately *you* must be the most resilient and the most driven.

Verifying that the five essential characteristics of an ideal student are in place, you are ready for your dissertation work. While you may start with all these in place, changes might occur which require your reconsideration of how your dissertation work influences your life. (For some, this means taking a break; for others, collaborating with their committee to create a schedule helps everything to stay on course. You will need to find ways to modify your ideals to align with a reality base.)

It is clear that much of your work will be done independently, so we turn to that topic next.

Your Dissertation Work

Your "work" is multidimensional, including conducting a research study *at the same time as* collaborating with a professional team, *at the same time as* living the rest of your life and meeting all of your responsibilities in other realms. There is a considerable amount of work which you will do independently. In the main, these activities will be: reading, planning, conducting your study, and writing it up. Clearly, thinking is at the center of all these activities. While each of them will be addressed individually here, there is a certain reciprocity among all these activities: your reading will lead to your planning and then your planning will result in additional reading, for example (see Figure 9.2). It should also be noted that you might start with any of the activities, but that ultimately your work will require all. And you may go back and forth between reading and writing many times. Eventually, these reciprocal and recursive activities result in the creation of a substantial research report called "Your Dissertation."

Reading

You will read voraciously and widely so that you become the most knowledgeable person in a specific domain. You will know what's been done, what's in process, and what directions your field is taking. This knowledge positions you to identify what needs to be done next. As you read a journal article, your inquisitive sense might be sparked by a recommendation "for future research," or you may devise a potentially more effective way of testing one aspect of a theory.

You will read dissertations completed at your institution for several reasons:

• to see topics which others have found interesting;

Figure 9.2   *The cyclical and recursive process: working independently on your dissertation*

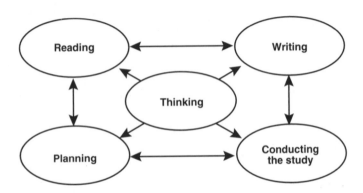

- to identify specific faculty interests;
- to get a sense of what a dissertation looks like in general; and
- to note all the components of an accepted dissertation.

You might specifically seek to read dissertations of recent graduates from your program or those sponsored by your chair to become informed about what they've done and perhaps become inspired by their example. You will read widely and deeply on your topic, noting a range of methods for data collection and data analysis adopted in these studies. While you are becoming familiar with what has been done, you are simultaneously considering how your study will be unique, contributing to the scholarship in your area of inquiry.

You should also read dissertations from other institutions so that you can recognize the common and unique characteristics of dissertations.[2] From your readings you may become interested in continuing a specific line of research connecting to your professional responsibilities. It is important to leave yourself open to such occurrences.

A frequent concern is: "When do I stop reading?" There is no easy response to the inquiry. Probably the most accurate answer is, "It depends." Let's say you feel as though you have read all there is to know about your topic. You are finding that the documents you are reading are all repeating the same issues you've discovered earlier in other pieces and the cited references are all familiar to you. Thus, you feel as if you are ready to move on to the next step which is probably writing a statement of your projected research problem.

As you start to write you may realize that there are gaps in your knowledge. And so, you return to do additional, but very targeted, reading. Thus, your reading and your writing become reciprocal processes in some respect. And you can document your progress through reflections on your multiple written drafts. As you read, there are several important organizational matters which will facilitate your research and writing:

- Make a bibliographic reference card for each document you look at. This may be in the form of a hard copy on an index card or stored as a set of computer records. Before you go any further than reading the title or the author's name, make a note of the following information:

  - Title
  - Author (include first and last names, and any initials)
  - Publisher
  - City and State of Publication
  - Date of Publication
  - Journal Volume Number and Issue Number
  - Pages of the Article or Chapter
  - Editor of Edited Volume
  - Library Call Number
  - Library (if you're using more than one library)

- This information should be archived in a database for your retrieval when: you want to access an article a second time; you want to verify that you have looked at this reference; you need to create your bibliography; you need to find out if you've seen anything by a particular author or in a particular journal; you want to refer to an article in your text and need the date of publication or the appropriate pronoun when referring to the author. Some people may find that keeping this file alphabetically will make it easier to locate materials. If stored as a computer database, you are likely to have a variety of ways of organizing this information, depending on your need at the moment. Computer software will format your information for a variety of style guides. While you will need to assure the accuracy of the text, the software certainly takes care of much of the nitty-gritty detail.
- Note the usefulness of the material once you have read it, thereby avoiding your return to documents you already know.
- Create numerous *topical note cards* for each text, placing a potential topic or category for ease of reference. Include notation of author and date on each card. Group these cards by topic; you may revise these topical designations as you progress in your understanding of issues.
- When copying a direct quotation from a published source, note the location of page breaks if a quotation extends over more than one page. Document the exact place in the text where a page ends, noting the word which ends the page (e.g. "last word on page, p. 5"). If a page break occurs where a word is divided, be cautious to note the precise letter which appears prior to the page break. At the end of the quotation, note all the page numbers ("pp. 5–6"). If you subsequently decide to use only one part of the text which you copied, you will not have to return to the original to determine the page where the quoted material appears. You will already know what text is found on each page. (Each researcher has a few pet strategies. Inquire from all the resources which surround you and are waiting to be tapped.) You never stop your reading. There are always new publications, and there is an infinite amount of information available which might be related to your topic. But you also need to be pragmatic. You make a judgment call when you decide you have read "enough," at least for the time being, allowing you to move along responsibly and productively.

Planning

Throughout the entire process you will be planning. You plan your research questions, your methods for collecting and analyzing your data, and the organization of your findings. Your planning will take several forms. You will:

- establish a productive mind-set;

- schedule your dissertation time, including times when you will have access to specific resources; and
- document your progress.

Establish a productive mind-set

Reduce the tension in your life, to free yourself to work on this project. Many outsiders will try to place pressure on you. You need to find a way to ensure that your own pressures do not add to this burden.

Respond to serendipitous insights by writing them down immediately. This advice might result in your jotting notes on a pad of post-its on your bedstead in the middle of the night while your eyes are closed. You will find it useful to return to these notes, clarifying the formation of the letters and words so that you will have a useful reminder when your scheduled time for working on your dissertation occurs.

By removing your headphones and moving away from the video and the computer, you will find that your mind continues working on your dissertation while you're doing other things such as walking to the train, taking the garbage out, or even watching the birds hop from branch to branch! Keep paper and pencil with you at all times.

Schedule your dissertation time

Establish your own schedule for tasks. Creating a checklist of all the steps in the process, you will be in a position to document where you've been and where you need to be heading. Thus, once you've identified your research focus, you need to write the specific question(s) which will guide your research, and you need to provide a rationale for your selection of this issue based on a critical review of the literature in your discipline. (You may create your own checklist using the one presented in Appendix E as a sample.)

Be flexible. Although you might have planned to work every day in a given week, other responsibilities may have encroached on that time. Don't focus on what did not happen. Find a way to make a reasonable schedule and keep to it. In fact, if your schedule calls for you to work on your dissertation every morning and you find that you suddenly have time one afternoon, some people would suggest that you *not* use that time for dissertation writing. Others would say, go with your instincts. Work on it whenever the mood strikes you, but be adamant about keeping to your personally drafted schedule as a minimum. Adjust your expectations and schedule realistically to accommodate your agenda and your responsibilities.

Take into account your access to the resources which you need to complete your project. For example, if your chair is taking a sabbatical leave, you will need to discuss plans for your progress during this time. Also, if the university library is scheduled to close for a month, you will need to find other resources, or reorganize your schedule. Find activities to pursue which will help *you* to progress.

Developing a productive setting

Perhaps a useful guiding principle is always to have a sense of your next step. Knowing where you are going will keep you task-oriented and focused on moving towards achieving your goal.

Document your progress

You may feel that, as one person expressed it, "I knew when I was at the beginning, but for what seemed a long time, I felt I was going in circles." To move beyond this feeling you will need to use your checklist to note where you've been and where you're trying to go. Although you will note that your activities (reading, planning, writing, etc.) recur in the process of research, you should also document progress in moving your research closer to its conclusion.

Conducting your Study

There are numerous excellent books on research methodology which should guide you in the process of conducting your study (see Appendix D for some suggestions). They will emphasize that there are two main parts to conducting to your study: collecting your data, and analyzing your data. As for collecting your data, you will probably be responsible for identifying a place to collect them, getting all the necessary approvals from the university and the research site, and creating the procedures to gather all the data which you need to conduct your study. You may create or select published interview questions, tests, and topics for discussion. You may also need access to videotape equipment, or permission to study at a specific site.

It is pragmatic to do some pilot or feasibility tests to work out the kinks in your plans, as well as to assure the likelihood that your procedures for collecting your data respond to your research question(s). If you are dependent on the audio-tapes collected during an interview, you will need to ascertain that the equipment and the setting will produce audible tapes. Many a study has gone awry when equipment failed, requiring the researcher to return to the site, or to find additional sites and participants to complete the study. Others have found that files with transcripts have disappeared from their computers at work. Be responsible for as much of your data collection as possible. Based on trial runs, you should revise your questions, your methodology, and your strategies for data collection.

When analyzing your data you are guided by the research processes you identified in your dissertation proposal. You are responsible for coding and processing your data, explaining your procedures and your rationale for choosing these strategies. You also have to deal with the credibility of your findings, explaining why the readers of your dissertation should believe that your findings are truthful, valid, and/or reliable.

Writing and Rewriting

You will find yourself writing and rewriting throughout the process of doing your dissertation. Look on your writing both as a way to document your current understanding and as a way to see where you need to direct your energies. Writing is probably one of the most difficult tasks we ask ourselves to do. Free yourself to start writing, recognizing that your first words, lines, even pages, may just be a warm-up for the more polished statements which will become your final text. Frequently writers get stuck trying to select an exciting title, or the perfect word, handicapping their flow of ideas. Most writers find it productive to get ideas down on paper initially, postponing for subsequent revisions the selection of the best word and the creation of a cohesive organization.

Writing is difficult, yet it is essential for you to make progress. The sooner you start writing, the more rapidly you are likely to progress. Discover your own writing style: can you work directly at a word processor? Do you feel more comfortable with some handwritten notes? Can you revise your word-processed text on screen, or do you prefer to work with printed text? Each person develops a style and works at simplifying it. Do not expect perfection at any time, particularly not at the beginning. Allow yourself to leave spaces where you will need to add information, and places where you can note vague understandings. But get started!

Keep all your drafts. It is possible that you may want to use some text which you discarded earlier. Having your old drafts will enable you to retrieve these texts. In addition, by comparing drafts, you are likely to note the changes in your organization and an expansion of your understanding of a phenomenon.

Some useful mechanical strategies:

- Date each draft.
- Focus initially on getting your ideas down. Gradually attend to revising your text into the format which is accepted for the final version. Postpone initially the concern for precise and concise presentation of information.
- Compile a list of all the sources you consult. You can always delete later.

As you create your text, you will want to emphasize where your study will add to extant knowledge. This may require that you identify a weakness in another person's study which you may be reluctant to do. Rather than explicitly making this judgment, it may be more effective to quote directly from the author of the study under scrutiny, allowing the published words to mark the problem. In this process, the reader criticizes the author's original words, without presenting an explicit criticism.

As the writer of your dissertation, you are both the guide and the interpreter of much information. Early on in your writing, you may not be clear about where you are going. Then, once you know what you have discovered, it is possible to present your findings as an informed guide. Thus, you will revise early drafts to reflect your new understanding. Rewriting is an essential element in your dissertation work and all polished writing.

Your writing may take place at home, at your office, at the university, at a library, or at a computer facility. Wherever you find yourself, make sure that you always work on diskettes. And create multiple copies on diskettes or a zip drive. Be cautious of saving on your hard drive. There seem to be mechanical and human gremlins who play with these objects, and can potentially destroy your work. Be in control of your work by being almost paranoid about it. Always have multiple copies of each document. When giving work to your committee for reaction, always keep a copy for yourself. When working on text, frequently back up on additional diskettes and/or as hard copy. You cannot back up too much! And then secure these copies in multiple sites.

The Other People in Your Life

While your dissertation will become a large part of your life, your home life and your work life are important as well. Each setting needs attention, and this adds to the pressures on doctoral students.

At Home

Home relationships become tense for many doctoral students. If you cannot find ways to accommodate your responsibilities at home with the demands of your doctoral program, you are likely to experience major angst. Spouses may feel abandoned or intimidated while doctoral students typically look to their families to support them through the tense times.

Hawley (1993) suggests, "As time-consuming as families are, they provide an anchor in the crazy world of doctoral study. They are your link with reality" (p. 149). Having a regular reality check is healthy for your soul, which you need to feed. You don't want to finish your degree and find you don't care about anyone and no one cares about you. Our lives are enriched by our friends and family. As you progress in your dissertation work, be mindful of others' feelings and find ways to include significant others in your newly evolving world while you continue living in theirs.

Many doctoral students find ways to balance the conflicting worlds of home and university by drawing on their spouse's expertise in completing the dissertation. Others share their checklists, documenting the numerous hurdles, and collaborate on strategies to allocate time. Knowing how long this activity will last is instrumental in obtaining cooperation and understanding. When the time line is unclear, inordinate pressures come to bear on the relationship. The non-student spouse or child, for example, may resent the seemingly unending process. This annoyance may show itself in interesting ways. Marilyn told me, "My husband taped a TV program over the data I collected at my school." Although she did not seem to interpret it as a malicious act, it might have been an unconscious one since it has been repeated many times in other settings.

Life goes on while you work on your dissertation. The draining of finances, the straining of relationships, and the vague requirements for completion contribute to untold tension. Margaret told me that she had the "worst fight of my marriage" on the day of graduation. These are predictable pressures which you must accommodate in some way. The entire process becomes a constant struggle for many students.

At Work

> Having a full-time job makes the process very frustrating because of the constant disruption and interruption in the process.

Try to find some connections between your doctoral program and your job. It is very possible that your work responsibilities will lead to the identification of your research problem. Let your co-workers and your supervisors know if you are "looking for a dissertation topic." One person noted, "My job changed, and so did my question." Ask to be included in conversations where topics related to your discipline are being discussed. When you are offered an opportunity to accept additional responsibilities, you can view this from several stances, as:

* reward for good work;
* respect for your work;
* an obstacle to increase the burdens in your life;
* a predictable sign of progress in a project; or
* competition for the time needed to work on your dissertation.

You will need to make a judgment and determine your response. Don't let others set your agenda. Constantly consider your options and your priorities. It is often advisable to take a short-term perspective, giving great energy to completing your dissertation while expecting that you will subsequently be in a mental and physical state to devote all of your energies and enthusiasm for new projects. It is wonderful to have choices. Once you are done with your dissertation, a whole new world of choices will open up to you. And so, let's get on to writing your proposal and completing your dissertation.

Notes

1 Quoted comments were provided by respondents to anonymous questionnaires, interviews and focus group discussions with doctoral students and completers at universities across the USA. For additional details about this study, see Appendix A.
2 *Dissertations Abstracts International*, a repository of most dissertations, is available in most university reference libraries. Journals and professional handbooks provide periodic summaries of recent dissertations. Review articles presented in journals, and some edited books, synthesize recent developments in your field, frequently suggesting future directions and recommendations for needed research.

Part III
Doing *Your* Study

10 Writing Your Dissertation Proposal While Designing Your Dissertation Research

I have changed ... in so many ways. I feel so much more confident about what I can do. I believe I can do almost anything!

Writing and defending a dissertation caused me to approach issues more critically.
(Quoted by Haworth, 1999, p. A13)

Writing your dissertation proposal prepares you for conducting your research and subsequently writing your dissertation. A dissertation proposal typically is comprised of several related sections. In many instances, the dissertation proposal has a proscribed format, including several chapters. The content of the proposal may include an explanation of the *rationale* for planning the study and a *design* for conducting the study. In some institutions this can be a relatively brief ten- to fifteen-page document, whereas in others it is lengthy, averaging seventy-five pages.

Writing the proposal takes a significant amount of time since most doctoral students are developing their ideas about their dissertation *concurrently* with their writing a document in acceptable form for institutional approval. Because the document includes components essential in conducting the research study, you may use the format as a preliminary outline for drafting plans for your research. Apprentice researchers typically write each section of the proposal, intending to revise it, based on professors' feedback. In the process of moving from section to section, you will refine your ideas, requiring your revision of earlier sections to present a consistent perspective. The multiple drafts enable you to contemplate important issues while becoming proficient at writing in the acceptable genre for your institution. This chapter offers a great number of details inherent in the writing of your dissertation proposal. From a "quick read" you will get the gist of the chapter. Since there are numerous *minute* details discussed, you will find it useful to return to each section as you progress in your own proposal writing.

I will discuss the purposes for writing a dissertation proposal first, and then proceed to discuss the content of the proposal, as well as typical steps towards approval of your proposal. While there are probably unique components to each institution's process and proposal form, the guidelines which follow are fairly representative of most program requirements.

Purposes for Writing a Dissertation Proposal

There are six major purposes accomplished by writing your dissertation proposal. In writing it, you:

- identify your specific research focus;
- create a group of faculty scholars who will guide your research apprenticeship;
- establish your research proficiencies;
- acquire proficiency in a writing style acceptable for your dissertation;
- draft early chapters of your dissertation;
- and prepare yourself for writing your dissertation.

Let's consider these purposes.

Identify your specific research focus In order to write your dissertation, you need a clear research agenda. Your research agenda is derived from your depth of knowledge of your "field," including your understanding of the theories which are guiding your discipline and the directions in which your discipline is moving. Your research typically either systematically *tests* one aspect of a theory, or generates data towards *theory-building* where there is no viable theory.

The dissertation research is intended to contribute to an on-going professional discussion. In each discipline there are debates about important issues. Your dissertation is intended to inform that dialog. Your dissertation proposal is your opportunity to present an "argument" acknowledging multiple perspectives while advancing a new perspective on the on-going discussion. Your focused presentation is intended to convince your readers that this proposed study is *worthwhile* doing and that you have the necessary *expertise* to conduct the study.

Create a group of faculty scholars Faculty with expertise in areas germane to your study direct your writing of your dissertation proposal. These professors nurture your learning and evaluate your work, eventually deciding when they believe it meets the university's standards.

As you progress you will give evidence of understanding another element in the dissertation process: your reliance on others. Some chairs want their doctoral students to be "humble," displaying their dependency on their mentor for progress in their dissertations. Others want students to be independent, utilizing all the resources available to them without overburdening the chairs. In most instances, students need to adopt multiple stances, depending on the stage they are at in the dissertation process and the preferences of the members of their committee.

Establish your research proficiencies   Since most doctoral students have limited experience in conducting research, particularly on dissertation scale, the dissertation proposal serves to validate the doctoral student's potential as a researcher. From this perspective, then, your preparation of the proposal is a quick immersion in research methodologies and problem finding.

Acquire proficiency in a writing style acceptable for your dissertation   The style of writing in dissertations is often disparagingly called dissertation-*ese*. While this style is unique, it is not universally valued. Many universities are more expansive in the styles which they accept. It is essential that you demonstrate your writing proficiency in the genre(s) acceptable at your university as part of the proposal writing process.

Draft early chapters of your dissertation   It is not unusual for many parts of the dissertation proposal to be included in your dissertation. Particularly in settings where the proposal is quite lengthy, students incorporate large parts of the proposal text in their dissertations.

Prepare yourself for writing your dissertation   Once you have succeeded in meeting the expectations for the dissertation proposal, you will have a clearer idea of the form, content, and procedures for completing your dissertation. In some respects you can view the proposal writing as a dry run for your dissertation writing.

Writing the proposal is a major step on the road to getting done with your dissertation. It provides students with the necessary tools for conducting dissertation research while assuring the university that the student has the appropriate knowledge and proficiencies for succeeding at this project.

Contents of the Dissertation Proposal

The dissertation proposal is a preliminary, scholarly document. It is preliminary to your dissertation. It is scholarly in that it follows the style guide adopted by a scholarly organization (e.g. the American Psychological Association or the Modern Language Association) and it presents an academic argument or position advancing your research as a potential contribution to knowledge. Each word is carefully chosen to convey precisely the intent of the writer. The organization clearly facilitates the reader's understanding of the major issues. The content impresses the academic community with the writer's breadth and depth of knowledge and with the importance of the proposed study to advance knowledge or understanding of a practice or a phenomenon.

The proposal typically contains four major components:

1   A descriptive title.
2   A statement of the research problem or question and the theoretical concerns to be addressed.

3   A presentation of studies and theories which are related to the proposed study.
4   An explanation of the procedures planned to conduct the proposed study.

Although these are listed as four separate parts, they are actually interdependent. The title of your proposal notes key issues which your study will investigate. The methods are influenced by the theories under investigation. The different parts may initially be written in isolation, but gradually they become directly linked. In the example given in Figure 10.1, a table of contents from a dissertation proposal, you notice the most significant terms appear in all the sections: "classroom discourse," "learning disabilities," and "learning." In many respects, your first drafts are times for clarifying the major issues. As you revise the several sections, you will create a consistent, coherent whole.

Typically, multiple drafts of a proposal are made, during which time the doctoral student becomes more precise about what will actually happen in the study, while simultaneously working toward an increasingly integrated presentation of the major theories and research which are guiding the project. This recursive process (going from one part of the proposal to another and returning again) will be an integral part of creating your final, polished dissertation proposal. We will consider the contents of each of the different sections.

While there are several different goals for conducting research (e.g. test a theory, build a theory, critique practice), there is usually only one format for the dissertation proposal. That format is most directly aligned with studies which are intending to test a theory. While this causes a problem for those who are conducting different types of study, chairs and their students have become resourceful in adopting the established style to their needs. For example, in studies which are intending to develop categories of analysis in the process of collecting data, dissertation proposals focus on possible and probable directions, noting that as the study progresses, additional decisions will be made. Some of these differences are noted in the chart below.

Characteristics of hypothesis-generating studies	Characteristics of hypothesis-testing studies
Tentative	Fixed
Evolves	Predictable
Speculative	Explicit
Responsive to setting	Predetermined

Figure 10.1   *Sample table of contents for a dissertation proposal*
Source: Levine (1993)

Proposal Title: Classroom Discourse with Students Labeled Learning Disabled

Chapter I: The Problem

    Statement of the Problem

    Theoretical Rationale

        Classroom Discourse

        Classroom Discourse and Theories of Learning

        Language and Learning

        Learning Theories for Students Labeled Learning Disabled

    Limitations of the Study

Chapter II: Review of the Literature

    Historical Perspectives on Learning Disabilities

    Educational Programs for Students Labeled Learning Disabled

    Classroom Discourse

        The Potential Influence of Peer Groups

        The Roles of the Teacher

        Classroom Discourse and Learning

Chapter III: Research Design

    The Setting of the Study

    The School

    The Classroom

    The Participants

        The Teacher-Researcher

        The Students

    Collection of the Data

        Videotaped Lessons

        Interviews

        Lesson Plans and Curriculum Plans

    Methodological Considerations

    Verifications and Validity

    Analysis of the Data

        Preliminary Processes for Developing Categories

        Categories Emerging from the Data

    Feasibility Study

REFERENCES

Writing your dissertation proposal

To understand the contents of dissertation proposals, carefully study at least two dissertation proposals for studies somewhat similar to your own. Your chair may be able to facilitate your access to their documents.

A Descriptive Title

The title of your proposal indicates the key issues which you are planning to investigate. Titles in hypothesis-testing studies typically identify the variables, along with the participant(s) or subject(s) in the study (e.g. "The Relationship of Teacher Efficacy and Organizational Variables in Special Education Referrals Among Inner-city Elementary Teachers"). Philosophical, critical, and hypothesis-generating studies usually state the research focus (e.g. "Opportunities and Obstacles in Bilingual Reading"). The title is closely connected to the other parts of the proposal. Although you will phrase a title for your study early in the writing of your proposal, you are likely to revise it as you proceed. Phrasing your title is a very important, preliminary step. It provides you with an easy anchor. You can reach out for your title page when you feel like you're loosing ground.

A Statement of the Research Problem or Question and the Theoretical Concerns to be Addressed

If you started thinking about possible topics early in your program, creating a growing list, you are now ready to revisit this list, eliminating questions which are not of great interest to you at this time. Discuss with faculty the ideas which are most compelling to you, seeking a sense of acceptable topics, important questions in your discipline, their relevance to *your* professional concerns, and their interest to potential faculty. It is easier to maintain your momentum when *you* have a passionate interest in your topic. In addition, be guided by topics suggested by professors, as discussed in Chapter 6.

It will be your responsibility to persuade your chair, and eventually the readers of your proposal, that the topic you have selected is compelling, in that it:

- arises from your comprehensive understanding of the current knowledge in your field;
- addresses a pivotal issue in your discipline;
- is doable; and
- is potentially significant.

The statement of your research problem typically includes three parts:

- a relatively brief discussion in which you present a "problem" in your academic discipline;
- a cohesive theoretical rationale; and
- a statement of the potential significance of the study.

The problem may be one of theoretical importance and/or it may have practical relevance. Your problem should be explicitly phrased: for example, "Since there is little knowledge about the writing of kindergarten children, the intent of my study is to describe the purposes for which kindergarten students write." This is followed by a brief discussion of the reasons why this is important to study, the length of time you will collect your writing samples, the location of the school, and the number of students to be studied. You may also offer some descriptions of data which may be included in your study, such as drawings with labels, name tags, etc.

To expedite your completion of this research and the receipt of your degree, you may want to pick a topic which is "do-able" in a brief time period. Longitudinal studies (following the same people for several years) typically take longer than "cross-sectional" studies (in which you choose people of different ages to represent growth over time).

A Presentation of the Studies and Theories which are Related to the Proposed Study

Following your statement of the problem, you will discuss the theoretical rationale. This section usually indicates the unique qualities of your study, which may include:

*   filling a theoretical or research gap in the discipline;
*   exploring an inconsistency in research findings; or
*   clarifying a conflict between theories.

In this section, the theory or theories which are connected to the "problem" are explained. You make a case for the importance of this topic based on the gaps in theories, the evolving knowledge, the need to test untested theories, and/or the conflicts between theories that are currently being discussed in your discipline.

Your theoretical rationale has several characteristics, in that it:

*   selects current, relevant, major theorists;
*   provides a historical evolution incorporating classical, seminal studies and theories which are repeatedly referred to in the studies which you value;
*   reflects the professional expertise available at your academic institution; and
*   contributes to the academic discipline, noting links between previous studies and your proposed study.

If a researcher is seeking to test the validity of a theory of language proficiency which has not been tested, the researcher may select one specific aspect of language, such as understanding ambiguous statements. The researcher presents an argument for selecting this particular aspect of language to study. The argument is derived from key issues in published studies and theories in the field of language. The researcher "makes a case" for studying the problem. There should be a rational or logical connection between the research problem and the theoretical discussion which follows.

The dissertation proposal for a hypothesis-testing study includes a discussion of the reasons for studying designated variables. Researchers select specific aspects of the theories to study in offering a rationale for focusing on these named variables. Frequently hypothesis-testing research questions are posed as "null hypotheses" which assume, for example, that there "is no statistically significant difference" between treatment A or treatment B. Some hypothesis-testing studies use directional hypotheses, predicting the direction presented in the theory which is being tested in the study. The theoretical rationale explains the reasoning behind the selection of the variables.

Some institutions expect that you will summarize the most important studies and theories. Others expect a more synthesized presentation wherein the candidate critiques what has been done as a basis for suggesting how the proposed study will both differ and benefit from what has already been done. Alternatively, your proposal might be topically focused, using themes which recur in the relevant literature to organize the multiple issues which are informing and influencing your investigation.

You may present a historical perspective on an evolving theory, explaining the foundations for the study on the basis of those documents which are frequently referred to as the "literature" of the profession. You may present studies which in some way are helpful in designing your study. If you can think of your study in terms of topics rather than theorists, for example, you may have a fruitful format for organizing your information. Reviewing the topics used to organize the theoretical rationale in dissertations, for instance, may provide you with useful organizational principles.

You will display your knowledge of your topic and your understanding of the nuances in the field in this section of your proposal. It is not unusual for doctoral students to feel overwhelmed. They have so much information, and need to present it to others in a coherent form. To get beyond this phase, look at other dissertations and look at other texts which you have been reading as examples of organized presentations. The group of topics for your dissertation are likely to be unique, but you might find some titles used in others' writings which may also serve your purposes, at least as a start.

The theoretical rationale section closes with a brief statement of the *potential significance of your study*. In non-technical terms you seek explicitly to persuade your readers both that this is the perfect time to do this study because it is likely to make an important contribution to your field, and that you are preeminently knowledgeable and proficient to conduct the study.

An Explanation of the Procedures Planned to Conduct the Proposed Study

In the procedures section you discuss your projected methods for collecting and analyzing the data which responds to your research question. This is an opportunity for you to be creative while illustrating the depth of your knowledge of the field. Drawing on all the studies which you have read, you will design a process to provide you with the best data and the best strategies for interpreting your data.

There are an infinite number of ways to do a study. Now is your chance to demonstrate your unique style, consistent with the criteria which have been established in your discipline. Although there may be numerous ways to proceed, time constraints will probably help to guide your selection of procedures which can be accomplished within a reasonable time period, perhaps adapting accessible resources.

It is important for you and your committee to visualize precisely what you are planning. In this way, your committee can help you to avoid problems while being assured that you know what you are doing. Some writers find it useful to consider this section as a recipe or a set of directions for others who wish to "replicate" your study.

A word of caution: it is important for you to recognize that you probably have the largest vested interest in this project, and it is your responsibility to make sure that everything works as *you* expect. (Even with your surveillance, there are likely to be glitches, but at least you will know about these immediately.) Have back-up plans in case your first choices don't work.

There are several sub-sections to address in the procedures section:

- data to be collected;
- procedures for collecting the data;
- procedures for analyzing the data;
- validity and reliability

In each instance, *prepare to explain your rationale for selecting the materials and/or processes in light of the theory or phenomenon under investigation.*

Data to be collected

In order to respond to your research questions, you will need data. It is your responsibility to identify the specific data which you plan to collect. See Figure 10.2 for typical data sources.

Procedures for collecting the data

Once you've identified *what* you will collect, you need to explain *how* you plan to collect it. If you are planning to study specific students reading a Shakespearean text, for example, you will need to explain the criteria you will use in selecting these participants, the number of participants, the setting in

Figure 10.2   *Typical data sources*

standardized test scores	participant-observer notes
writing samples	demographic information
journal entries	researcher developed tests
notes or field notes	interview questions
narrative vignettes	videotapes of classroom interactions
published texts	artifacts (contemporary or historic)
surveys	transcripts

which you will collect the data, and the procedures you will create to document their reading. You may videotape them as they sit in the classroom, you may read the notes which they create in their texts or in their journals, and/or you may sit in on a discussion and oral readings of the play. Whatever you are planning to do must be explicitly detailed, for example by providing a diagram of the placement of the video camera if it is going to be used.

The issue of sample size will probably be addressed in your proposal. You probably want a "just right size" group, rather like Goldilocks when she was visiting in the three bears' home. If your sample is too large, it may become unwieldy. On the other hand, if you are seeking to utilize statistical analysis to test a hypothesis, for example, you must have an adequate sample size to "run" the specific statistical tests appropriate for your data. A sample that is too small may disappear with time, leaving you with no participants. When considering the number of initial participants, you may want to contemplate the possibility that drop-outs from your study may decrease your initial data pool. *All researchers* make a compromise between depth and breadth. Some choose to have more informants with limited data. Others elect to have few participants with a large quantity of data collected from these individuals. The decision must be made in collaboration with your committee, guided by the traditions established in your discipline.

If you are planning to transcribe video- or audio-tapes, you will want to think about procedures to ensure the accuracy of the transcript. If someone else will transcribe your tapes, explain how you will monitor the process. If students are placed in groups, identify criteria used in placing them randomly, in "equivalent" groups that are consistent with the theory being studied or in naturally occurring groups, for example.

PILOT TESTING OR FEASIBILITY STUDIES

If you are planning to develop an instrument or an interview protocol, you will want to determine its usefulness by pilot testing it with a smaller number of participants. After piloting your instrument, you will be able to revise and refine parts to create an ideal instrument for your study.

Based on a review of their audio-taped pilot interviews, researchers frequently find it useful to strengthen their ability to pose questions spontaneously in interviews. Others see that participants are bored and seek to find more interesting ways to obtain their data. Still others determine that the projected survey is too long, and that if they asked fewer but more highly focused questions, they would get the same data. Pilot testing is a very important aspect of the research process.

If you are planning to use any technology, it is useful to experiment with the equipment and to become proficient in working all its parts. The frequency of problems highlights the need for back-ups: have two tape recorders running simultaneously, for example. If you have technicians working with you, become knowledgeable about all the equipment which they are setting up. You never know when they will get sick, or you will need to stay longer than originally scheduled. Try to be as autonomous as possible, to avoid the possibility of being left without the essential data for your study.

Experienced researchers pilot all the components of a study. In this process they gain proficiency in handling all the parts while having the opportunity to create a process that is smoother, easier, and less disruptive for participants. Pilot studies typically are compressed, mini-studies, with smaller sample groups and a shorter time period, but comprehensive in experimenting with all the elements of the process. There are many advantages to doing a pilot. You get:

- a rehearsal to see how you will perform;
- confirmation that the processes will work;
- assurance that the materials you collect are the ones you need;
- an opportunity to experiment with procedures for analyzing the data; and
- an opportunity to revise your procedures as needed.

Despite these advantages, there is no guarantee that everything will work perfectly during your major study. However, by piloting, you do have a stronger chance that you will at least eliminate the major obstacles in your study, and that this will provide you with confidence to make the needed adjustments when conducting your major study.

There is an additional dimension in data collection for you to consider. Institutions are charged by the federal government with guaranteeing that participants in research studies are not harmed. This is an important ethical issue which some researchers neglect to consider. An interdisciplinary review panel meets periodically to review all research designs for projects sponsored by the university, those conducted by professors as well as those designed by students. This review typically takes place at least four times a year. Prior to starting your study, the Human Subjects Review Board reviews and evaluates if you are "intervening" in the lives of your participants in a harmful way. The board may offer suggestions or additional requirements which need to be addressed prior to initiating your study.

LIMITATIONS

Regardless of how carefully you plan your study, there will be "limitations" on the generalizability of your findings to other settings. These limitations are sometimes explicitly acknowledged. For example, the time during which you collected your data may have been for one year and it's impossible to predict what would happen in any other year. You may have conducted a cross-sectional study, and you cannot make any guarantees about the accuracy of the predictions for these particular participants' development. These are considered limitations on the interpretation of the findings. All studies have limitations, since no inquiry can address every possible dimension.

Procedures to analyze the data

After you have collected your data, you need procedures for analyzing them. All data are analyzed quantitatively to some degree. Those studies which utilize statistical tests of "significance" in researching the frequency of responses, for example, typically report these with a pre-established level of "confidence." The statistical test is predicted to be accurate for a certain per cent of the population. Thus, a finding at the .01 level suggests that the researcher can have confidence that 99 times out of 100, this same result will obtain with a similar population. Theoretically, in one case in a hundred it will not. Researchers are always cautioned that "statistical significance" is only one type of significance.

It is not unusual for doctoral students to seek the advice of a statistical consultant in the process of planning and implementing their studies. Some doctoral students warn that over-dependence on these experts handicapped them at their oral defenses, leaving them with verbatim quotes to offer in response to potential inquiries. These students wished they had a stronger command of the statistical processes when they needed to provide explanations at their orals.

Other ways of numerically analyzing data include determining means, modes, medians, rank orderings, and percentages. Reputable researchers select the analytical processes which respond to the initial research question(s). Be wary of advice to focus on the data which will yield interesting and/or significant statistics. Statistics, like all rubrics for analysis, need to offer "impartiality" in the analytical process. Avoid seeking statistical significance in lieu of addressing the original research questions.

Researchers may establish categories derived from their data, or they may use previously identified, predetermined categories. The decisions are based on the identified purpose of the research. If the research is intended to test a specific theory, then there are probably predetermined variables which need to be studied. On the other hand, if the study is intending to explore new territory, to contribute to theory building, then there is a need to be more open-ended in the analysis, responding to what is collected, and creating categories directly and exclusively from those data. (See, for example, Table 10.1

which is an early list of categories which Lillian Masters developed in writing her dissertation.)

Some researchers prefer to create categories from a "naturally occurring" phenomenon, establishing a system for representing the researcher's or the participants' perspectives on the most significant events and activities. In such studies, the responsible researcher clearly describes the procedures adopted in analyzing the data with elaborate definitions and descriptions. These details enable readers to individually assess the persuasiveness of the cases presented. Most researchers identify multiple ways of interpreting the data, thereby providing different lenses on the same information.

Researchers frequently find it useful to present the data graphically, using tables or figures. Particularly with the availability of computers and word-processing programs with graphic capabilities, the possibility for accommodating this practice is more realistic. The dissertation proposal may include samples of projected tables and figures presenting the information collected during the pilot study. This graphic presentation of data powerfully represents your findings in a picture which you then explain and refer to in the text.

VALIDITY

A concern for all researchers is the "validity" or truthfulness of the procedures used in the study. At this moment in time, the issue of validity is rather contro-versial in the research community (see, for example, LeCompte and Goetz,

Table 10.1 *Preliminary categories for analysis: a sample*

Potential category	Example	Definition
Reviewing	Tutor: "It sounds like you're doing what you were doing before ... making the story with the words."	*Reviewing* re-examines old information
Explaining	Tutor: "Like, like the words don't necessarily have to pertain to the story ... the girl doesn't have to run or she doesn't have to 'desire,' she doesn't have to 'leave,' maybe ... uhm, she was walking and the 'leaves' fell from the tree ... You know they don't necessarily have to describe her ... they can be part of the environment."	*Explaining* uses strategies offer varying interpretations
Suggesting	Tutor: "Like you could explain why it is you think that shows ... that the rocket is a little too into himself. You can explain why ... like when you read it ... you felt like ... like whatever gave you that impression?"	*Suggesting* advances ideas or offers new information

Masters (1997)

1982; Howe, 1998; Howe and Eisenhart, 1990; Richardson, forthcoming; and Wittrock, 1986). For instance, when there is a careful match among the theory being tested, the data collected, and the research question, there is construct validity – one important type of affirmation that your study has been carefully designed and implemented. Since one of your major concerns in conducting this study is to convince experienced researchers that this is quality research, you will want to provide clear evidence of the validity of the decisions you made in planning and conducting it. You want to provide assurance that you have complied with accepted research practices, discussing, for example, the reliability and validity or the truthfulness of all the procedures you followed in designing your study.

Another way to establish the validity of your methodology is to seek expert evaluation. You will want to respond to suggested revisions, either following the advice offered, or rejecting it. Your correspondence is frequently included in an appendix to your proposal. An explanation of all the steps you create to validate your study promotes respect for the quality of your research.

Steps Toward Approval of Your Proposal

There are numerous steps which mark you progress toward approval of your proposal. You will probably want to include each of these in your personal checklist and note when each has been fulfilled (see Appendix E).

Once your committee has confidence in your proposal, there is likely to be a formal proposal hearing. With an approved proposal in hand, you are ready for two things:

1 *Celebrate your major accomplishment.* One outcome of this review is a written approval which you should preserve in a safe place. This statement certifies the acceptance of your proposal by university reviewers. The approval theoretically signifies a commitment between the university and the student to support the completion of your project, providing you adhere to all the university's rules, such as registering each semester. But there are no guarantees. Complete your degree requirements as rapidly as possible to avoid new rules and expectations which inevitably accompany new administrations or faculty changes. Celebrate your progress – and ...

2 *Get on with the next phase of your work* – conducting your study!

11 Conducting Your Study

> By thinking of it as small parts – theoretical rationale, research design, etc. – I was able to divide the project into smaller, more manageable units and thereby was able to reduce the pressure on myself, and make it possible to see progress on this immense project.

> One thing the dissertation forced me to do was to reflect on what I was doing. This time to reflect was a gift.

With your committee's approval, you are now ready to "do your study." This is a most exhilarating time in the research process. It is at this point that you are able to use your unique talents, experiences, and knowledge. Your organizational skills ease your way as you both orchestrate this large-scale study and insure that you have the documentation you need to write it up. Now is the time when you discover the answer(s) to your research questions.

Being mindful that you are responsible for establishing your own schedule, you will create a time line, noting all the activities which need to be done, and giving adequate time for each step. As you make this list you will identify several activities which may be accomplished simultaneously. For example, when you send out questionnaires to one group of participants, you may schedule and conduct interviews with other participants. There is always something that can be done. Do not allow one day to go by without doing *something*. Your schedule keeps you in focus, as long as you revise it to reflect the real progress you are making and the added elements which need to be completed in your study. Expect that your initial projections will be revised. Don't allow any curve balls to stop you. They may cause you to take a new perspective, but keep a positive attitude, finding ways to *succeed*.

You will have the greatest control over the quality and the progress of your study if you personally take on responsibility for each part. Keep careful notes of all your activities as you collect and analyze your data, such as interview schedules, drafts of survey instruments, and analytical categories. These notes will be invaluable when you describe each step that you took in the research process.

There are three major activities integral to the process of conducting your study:

Conducting your study

- collecting and storing your data;
- analyzing your data; and
- interpreting your findings.

Although we will discuss these separately, these are interdependent components of your study as noted in Figure 11.1. There are times, for example, when you may analyze some of your data while you are still collecting further data.

Collecting and Storing Your Data

In your proposal you identified data which you expected to collect and use in conducting your study. Your data may take many forms. Depending on the focus of your study, you may collect a range of materials. For example:

census reports	unpublished documents
statistical tables	test results
interview questions	handwritten journals
field notes	survey responses
transcripts	published articles and letters
photographs	video-tapes
personal letters	parental approvals

You will need to establish systematic procedures for collecting and storing these data so that you can find them when you need them.

Collecting your Data

As you start your study you need access to all the materials which you have identified. The collection process may take the form of visiting libraries and/or identifying human participants. If you are planning to enlist the cooperation of others in your data collection (through interviews, responses to surveys, or the like), you need to find effective ways to accomplish this. Remember that the people who are your participants are helping *you*. There's probably nothing "in

Figure 11.1 *Conducting your study: a cyclical process*

it" for them except for the feeling that they are helping you, and/or the research community. Your recognition that your study is dependent on getting good data from these respondents will be evident in the ways in which you accommodate your respondents' priorities. Some suggestions for encouraging participation in your study are noted below.

Suggested strategies for gathering responses

- Keep the time needed to a minimum.
- Inform people of the time this is likely to take.
- Arrange a time that is convenient for your participants.
- Provide instructions which are easily understood.
- Insure anonymity and confidentiality where possible.
- Invite assistance from those concerned with the same issue you are studying, such as members of your professional organization.
- Note in your invitation the names of people on your committee who are respected by your potential informants.
- Expect that only about 50 per cent of the group of potential participants may respond.
- Limit the number of participants needed.
- Seek assistance from people you have helped.
- Provide a stamped, self-addressed envelope, when appropriate.
- Follow up on the telephone, by snail mail, or by e-mail.

Ultimately you must find a way to get people to respond. Without data, your study cannot go forward. If you run into problems, your committee and your program colleagues are excellent resources for addressing these concerns.

If you need to develop a questionnaire for a survey or interviews, you may find useful resources in other dissertations, published reports of related studies, conference presentations, or the like. There are also books written on interview strategies (see Appendix D for suggestions). Your study will be enhanced by pilot-testing your materials. It is also useful to audio-tape and then critically review your potential questions. Try to simplify your procedures for your participants.

Recent studies are increasingly collecting data on video-tapes and subsequently transcribing some of the verbal interactions. At the present time there are some software programs which may assist you in transcribing your data. But they will not replace your keen attention to the exact words uttered by your participants. Transcribing is laborious, time-intensive, and frustrating. It is also illuminating and fascinating. If you maintain field notes during the actual taping, and transcribe your tapes fairly soon after recording, you will find it easier to clarify seemingly chaotic data than if many months have elapsed or if you are absent from the taping experience. The video-tape and field notes are "raw" data, whereas the transcript is derived *from* your initial data. Each transcript represents a specific perspective. As you create your transcripts and decide what to include, be conscious of your selections and exclusions, and be ready to explain these decisions in your dissertation and at your oral examination.

While you are collecting all your data, you want to be as cautious as possible about restricting your influence on the activities. You want to maintain a neutral, explorer's stance, seeking to discover something new as you collect your data.

Storing Materials

Establish one place to store all your materials, a place no one else will disturb. As you engage in your data collection and analysis, you are likely to create numerous stacks of papers. You may have books and journal articles from the library, blank questionnaires, responses to surveys, new and recorded audio- and video-tapes, field notes, essays written in classes, pre-publication articles, e-mail from experts across the nation, conference papers, and equipment. The more cautiously you store these materials, the more likely it is that you will be able to retrieve them when you want them.

You will also need to find ways to categorize the materials you are accumulating. You might place all your completed questionnaires in one box, and the names and addresses of people surveyed in a second box. Your computer diskettes may be organized chronologically, noting the data collected in the first three months of your study on Diskette #1 and that collected in the second three months on Diskette #2. One set of back-up diskettes may be stored near your computer, a second set placed on your living-room bookshelves, a third back-up in the form of your zip drive may be carried in your backpack. And of course, keep hard copies as well. *Be paranoid: store your data in many places.*

> Conducting the actual study can be exciting, as well as frustrating. It can be exciting if the researcher has organized the procedures for conducting the study and has enlisted the help of persons to assist in collecting the data. Even the most organized and well-planned study does not always go as anticipated, but good organization can help things move smoothly. It is very important that the researcher set deadlines for receiving data. There must be some contingency for retrieving data that are not received by that deadline. Some researchers may have a telephone committee to remind people to return data. Others may send out letters as reminders. Of course, much of this will depend on the type of research being conducted. When experimental research is done, the experimenter has more control over the situation. When descriptive-survey research is done, this is not the case.

> It is not unusual to find oneself changing deadlines when the data collection is not proceeding as anticipated. Recording the data as they are collected helps tremendously during this time.
>
> (Smith, 1982, pp. 40–1)

You want to secure all the raw data which you collect at least until your dissertation has been approved. These data are irreplaceable. With your data in hand, you are prepared for the next step: analyzing and interpreting your data, the focus of the next chapter.

12 Analyzing and Interpreting Your Data

I discovered the idea of making a calendar and placing the events on it *myself*; it was my very own idea. My chair hadn't given it to me at all. This was so exhilarating.

I began to believe that I could write something worthwhile in an interesting manner – something longer than a report or an essay.

Once you have collected all of your data, your next step is to "make sense" of the separate pieces of accumulated information. All of the data which you have collected are frequently called "raw" data because they are untouched by you. These "raw" data may be standardized test response sheets, tape recordings of interviews, or unpublished letters. You will need to make inferences from these discrete pieces of information as you analyze your data.

Before you go any further, I must emphasize the need to clarify your roles with your chair, since there are significant variations in how the next steps evolve. In many situations you will work closely with your chair, collaborating on your progress in analyzing your data. Some chairs want to participate in every step of the process. Others expect that you will work totally independently. In the former situation, you take on the role of an advanced apprentice, gaining confidence in your skills as a researcher while your chair guides your development. If your chair prefers to let you do it alone as part of your induction into the research process, you may create settings where you are able to talk about questions, clarify your procedures, and generally get useful support and guidance as you pursue this part of your research. You may find yourself enlisting the assistance of a dissertation consultant and/or independent researcher. You may go it alone. Take heart in the knowledge that others have succeeded before you. If they could do it, you can too!

The culture of your university, your program, and your chair, will dictate your role. Try to be as protective as possible of your own sanity while finding ways to develop expertise as an independent researcher. Your collegial support group reduces your isolation while building your confidence, as you explore strategies for making sense of your data.

Many students become overwhelmed at this point, not knowing how to organize their activities, what needs to be done first, or how to proceed to the point of obtaining "outcomes" or findings. They frequently comment that they are "drowning in their data." Basic advice is *divide and conquer*. Establish a sequence of several steps, systematically addressing the first step, then moving on to the next step. In this way, you can track your progress and know where you are headed. Refer to the checklist in Appendix E as a guide to creating your own schedule.

It is essential that you keep an open mind in the process of analyzing your data, remembering that research is conducted to *discover*, not to prove. You will need to look carefully at all of the data, seeking to uncover important insights into the phenomenon which you are researching. Subsequently you will synthesize all your data sources, creating a more holistic and integrated set of information which is frequently labeled "findings." The procedures you use to accomplish this analysis need to be explicitly documented and directly connected to your research questions.

Preliminary Organization of your Data

Your first task in responding to research question #1 (and all subsequent ones) is to convert the discrete pieces of data into a manageable, informative database. There are some preliminary steps which will get you started on your analysis. You may not need to wait until you have collected all of your data to start. If you have collected some data, you probably can start your analysis, or at least establish procedures for organizing your data beyond the top of your desk. Paper files and computer databases are two important organizing resources. Into these numerous files you may place a variety of information, such as:

* standardized test answer sheets;
* coded answer sheets;
* scored standardized test answer sheets using explicit criteria, typically the publisher's established correct responses;
* scores of your participants on the standardized test;
* topics discussed on essays;
* summaries of audio-taped classroom lessons;
* copies of your original data;
* descriptions of software programs available in the technology laboratory.

Remember to make copies of all your materials, and place these copies where they will not be touched by others. You never know when a disaster will strike, causing you to need to refer to your back-ups.

Starting Your Analysis

Your experience with your pilot or feasibility studies provides an excellent basis for designing your initial attempts at analysis in your major study. In your pilot study, you progressed from the separate pieces of data to making inferences, and then reviewing additional evidence to, for example, confirm or revise your inferences. One issue should be very clear: *the more familiar you are with your data, the better your analysis will be.*

If you ask others to assist in coding your data, transcribing your data, or in entering your data into the computer, you will not have as deep a familiarity with your data as those who accept responsibility for all these steps. Limited familiarity will influence the length of time it may take to identify important findings. If you ask others to assist you, review their work with a fine tooth-comb, assuring yourself of the accuracy of what they have done while becoming informed about all of your data yourself.

Your ability to quote verbatim from your data will lead you to know the patterns and the aberrations (e.g. an unusually filled-in bubble sheet). This information will help you to look at your data through more knowledgeable lenses, and thereby lead you to make more insightful discoveries. While you are learning your data "by heart" you do not want to drown in them. This problem is potentially acute in studies that utilize qualitative analysis.

The first goal in analyzing your data is to *reduce* the information you have collected to a manageable database, grouping your information in useful ways. There are numerous ways for you to make your data manageable. You will access your data more rapidly by reducing the number of papers you need to refer to. From the large stack of papers which contain your "raw" data find ways to synthesize or distill the information into a smaller set of notes which characterize your total data. You want to accomplish this reduction without losing the *qualities* which are integral to your total data set. This reduction process potentially includes creating categories which describe your data by identifying common qualities or patterns. Or you may compare one set of data (e.g. test scores) with another set of data (e.g. grade point average). *Your study is only as good as the data which you have to analyze and the care you take in analyzing them.*

Why is Explicit Documentation Important?

Exemplary studies provide sufficient information to enable a reader of the study to envision all the steps which the researcher followed. By providing a window into your procedures in analyzing the data, you assure your readers of your dispassionate, impartial analysis, suggesting that others following the same procedures would come up with similar findings. Thus, your documentation includes examples of both the data which are informing your study and the procedures which you used to analyze these data, transforming the separate pieces of information into a cohesive response to the research question(s).

This documentation is initially most useful as you review the procedures you implemented. Your notation of each step will allow you to consider possible oversights, gaps, and inconsistencies. By reviewing these notes, then, you can critique your own procedures prior to presenting them to your committee.

When professional colleagues are able to follow your line of reasoning, they have a basis for valuing the credibility of your study. If they have difficulty following your thinking due to a sketchy presentation of procedures, for example, they may have reservations about the way in which they will value your study. When they can visualize your procedures, they are more likely to consider your analysis credible.

Another reason for providing careful, step-by-step documentation of your procedures is to give other researchers, who may seek to replicate your study, access to your procedures. The aggregation of similar studies is one way in which theories develop or are strengthened. The more people know about your precise procedures, the more likely it is that others will consider using the same or similar procedures. In this way, your study may become a model for other studies, a wonderful contribution to the research community and an implicit affirmation of the value of your work.

To accommodate the concern for explicit documentation, you will find it useful to make careful notes of all the steps you go through in your process of analysis. This includes even the ones which you subsequently decided were dead ends. Your explanation of each of these decisions conveys a sense of care for your analysis and a sense of openness to your readers, again promoting the credibility of your interpretations.

You will employ a wide range of strategies to make sense of your data, drawing on three different domains:

1 Your direct experiences with your pilot study and/or your feasibility study.
2 Your understanding of procedures implemented in other studies.
3 General strategies adopted in the research tradition you are following.

Preliminary plans for your data analysis are frequently identified in your proposal. If you believe your initial plans were ill-conceived, you may need to redraft your proposal, obtaining approval from your committee for the changes. Alternatively, you may complete your study, explaining your rationale for revising your plans. Local norms may influence your decisions in this case.

Direct Connection to Your Research Questions

One way to begin your data analysis is to refer to your initial research questions which are clearly stated in your proposal. It is not unusual for students to forget about these, yet they are really important keys to your analysis. These questions usually identify what you need to analyze.

If you have multiple questions, you probably will find it easier to focus your attention first on one question. Identify the data which will inform your understanding of the issues implicit in question #1, for example. After you have completed a systematic analysis of data to respond to question #1 you may follow the same strategies with question #2, and so on, until you have organized all of your data by the research questions. This process is helpful in that it focuses your attention on one sub-set of your study. It frequently enables you to study more manageable data sets sequentially rather than simultaneously.

Thus, if you are looking at teachers' and students' perceptions of learning, you may first analyze your data from the teachers. After you have completed your review of the "teacher data," you may start on the students' data, applying the insights and expertise you developed in your first go-around'. Subsequently your review of teachers' data may incorporate the new insights you developed.

Throughout the process of analyzing your data be cautious of losing sight of the forest by focusing on individual trees. Connect each analytical process with a research question and multiple databases, insuring that you are not analyzing in isolation from your intended goal. Documenting your analytical processes in written notes both provides "grist for the mill" when you are ready to write your section on the processes you implemented, and promotes your understanding of what you have done and what else you might want to try. This effect of writing is so subtle that one respondent commented:

> I didn't see the writing as analyzing the data. I saw it as writing. And yet, now I can talk about my study and analysis, *not* my writing. There were moments during the writing process, when data analysis led to the discovery of insights. While much of the dissertation writing process was measured and slow-going, it was moments of discovery that led to spurts of exhilaratingly insightful writing. These analytical discoveries propelled the dissertation process forward.

Reducing Your Data

You need to transform your raw data into a format that will facilitate your analysis. This transformation may take several steps. You may note the presence or absence of specific words. You may note the number of correct responses. You may create a verbal transcript from a video-tape. These are all "first-level" analyses. You will need to work on each of these further, from a quantitative and/or a qualitative perspective. This process is frequently referred to as *reducing your data* because you will create groupings and combine separate sheets of paper from each subject, creating, for example, a single page with all the information you need.

The analysis of your data may take many forms, some of which may utilize technology. You may tally your responses by hand, or access a computer program with coded answer sheets. You may also select time-intensive human interrogation of the data to discover what you have found.

Finding Patterns in Your Data

Whether you are analyzing your data from a qualitative or a quantitative standpoint, you will look for patterns in your data. There are numerous excellent resources to guide your analytical processes. Selected references are listed in Appendix D. As you go through this intense process, try to remember that you will need to offer expansive explanations for all the decisions you make, both in your dissertation and at your oral defense. Some of these decisions may be about the statistical tests which you have selected. Others may focus on the processes you implemented in identifying patterns of response. As you become conscious of the decisions you are making, ask yourself to explain your rationale. If you are as critical of your own responses as your committee and external readers may be at your orals, you will be preparing for the predictable questions which will occur as you "go public" with your study.

Quantitative Strategies

Quantitative analysis typically refers to counting specific "units of analysis," as designated, for example, in your research question. In quantifying your data, you may find it useful to create a series of tables. Each table might note such data as the individual scores by grade or number of words in each essay. Data displays might include:

- tabulating the number of responses to each question;
- tabulating the number of correct responses to each question;
- listing the frequency of appearance of topics addressed in documents;
- listing scores by age or grade level;
- tabulating the number of respondents who offered each answer;
- comparing numerical data across events or participants;
- or comparing scores on a standardized test to scores on a researcher-created examination.

You might ask, "How do I know when to stop my data analysis?" The response is fairly straightforward in studies which identify a statistical test as the focus: for example, that there is no statistical difference between the scores on the SAT-history test of students who wrote a two-minute quick-write everyday in history class and those who did not. Depending on such issues as your sample size, you will select an appropriate statistical test. Completing the statistical tests may include graphing data and translating the numbers into visually informative graphs and charts.

It is not unusual for "outside experts [to] use more elaborate statistical procedures than are appropriate." Your dissertation is typically a first-level research study. Usually doctoral students are not expected to be as proficient as experienced researchers who may have conquered more sophisticated analytical processes. *Draw on university resources and check with your committee. Don't have the consultant act as a shadow committee.*

> The computer printouts may look like Greek to one who does not understand statistics, but to a statistician there is usually no problem. ... Sometimes the printouts do not have the complete program. One student

discovered, after several tries, that she had used the wrong program to analyze her data. Somewhere along the way, someone had suggested the wrong program and she had to go back to the drawing board to determine an appropriate program. If any phase of the process can be downright frustrating or confusing, it is this phase. One very simple error can cause one to lose a lot of time.

(Smith, 1982, p. 41)

Qualitative Strategies

Qualitative strategies usually focus on identifying frequently occurring phenomena. These phenomena are often called patterns of behavior. The behavior may be verbal or nonverbal. Qualitative researchers will frequently design scoring rubrics which characterize the specific data which were collected in their study. Typically the researcher develops unique categories through a series of cyclical processes, reducing the categories to both discrete and representative patterns found in the range of data collected.

Sample patterns may include:

* the range of topics discussed in the journal entries;
* samples of each topic discussed in the journals;
* typical participant responses to a short-answer test;
* participant actions in different settings;
* interactions in different settings; or
* language used in different contexts.

When doing a hypothesis-generating study you will find patterns, repetitions, commonalities. These are not simply repeated words, but concepts and/or processes which recur in your data, and hypothetically predictable in a larger and more random data pool. Some researchers use computer software such as *Ethnologue* and *Nud-ist* (Nonnumerical Unstructured Data-Indexing, Searching and Theorizing). These programs are intended to facilitate the process of data analysis by searching for specific words or phrases. While these programs do provide support for developing graphs and charts of repeated words and groups of words, they do not have the human capacity to identify synonymous words, for example. If the purpose of your study is to note the frequency of specific word choices, these tools may be very useful for you. In much of qualitative research the goal is to note the intent of the speaker or writer, which makes the applicability of such programs to qualitative studies more limited.

The patterns represent both a quantitative element and a qualitative element in the research. The patterns may be identified, for example, because of their frequent occurrence in the data. The qualitative component of these patterns may be realized, for example, in the presentation of typical samples of the phenomenon under investigation.

Interpreting Your Findings

> One major problem at this point becomes that of the researcher making more claims for the research than can be supported by the data. It is important to make inferences and generalizations, but unsupported generalizations and claims must be avoided.
>
> (Smith, 1982, p. 41)

It is important for you to keep three components of your study in mind as you interpret your findings:

1 Your initial research questions.
2 Your sample (with its limitations).
3 Your data analysis.

You want to answer your initial research questions within the context of the specific sample you focused on in your data collection. If your study was initially intended to test a hypothesis, your study should report the results of that testing. A typical outcome is the support of the original hypothesis or the lack of support of that hypothesis. Either finding is important.

If your study supported the original hypothesis (if it was a positive directional hypothesis supporting a particular theory, for example), this finding suggests the robustness of the theory which you were testing. On the other hand, if your study fails to support the original, hypothesis, that does not mean that this theory is invalid. Nor does it mean that your study was not good. Rather, the theory may, for example, apply to a sub-set of our population instead of being universally applicable. All carefully crafted research provides us with important information which allows us to have greater confidence in a theory, or which encourages us to re-think that theory more carefully. Either way, it provides us with useful information.

Knowing What You Found

Your goal in conducting this analysis is to figure out what you have found. You will scrutinize your data, interrogate your data, in the hopes of discovering what your data mean, or more precisely, what meaning *you* can make of your data.

When conducting tests of statistical significance, do not dismiss findings which are not "statistically" significant. Statistical significance is one way of identifying a potentially important finding. Researchers who equate *statistical* significance with significance *per se* may have lost sight of the true purpose of research. All findings are potentially useful and significant, regardless of whether they are "statistically significant."

In your roles as researcher and writer of your research report, you will want to find ways to understand your data, comparing sub-sets of your data, comparing your data with other studies, and comparing your data with the theories which contributed to your study's design. These comparisons may be displayed graphically, providing your readers with a context in which to interpret your findings. The adage that "one picture is worth 1,000 words," is useful to remember in this regard.

As you analyze your data, you may create some figures or tables to display your data in such a way that your readers will clearly see the issues which you are discussing. These graphic organizers are distinguished from one another by the American Psychological Association APA:

- *Tables* are typeset, rather than photographed from artwork supplied by the author. Tables are frequently used to present quantitative data.
- *Figures* are typically used to "convey structural or pictorial concepts." The types of figures can vary: graphs (line graphs, bar graphs, circle or pie graphs, scatter graphs, and pictorial graphs), charts, dot maps, and drawings. A figure may be a chart, graph, photograph, or a drawing: "Any illustration other than a table is called a figure" (APA, 1994, p. 141).

A few samples may prime your mind to think of informative ways to present your data. Look over the preceding chapters, noting the ways in which tables and figures clarified concepts and issues. Contemplate similar data presentations from your analysis of your own data.

As you become more familiar with your data and your findings start to emerge, you will find it useful to create a few such visual presentations. These graphic images will contribute to your understanding of your data, and thereby lead you to identify your unique "findings." They will also enable your readers to envision your findings. Readers of dissertations are frequently drawn to such displays of information, which typically synthesize the key findings of the study. They may subsequently read the text which accompanies the drawings. Alternatively, they may request your verbal explanation as a way to engage you in conversation about your study at pre-oral conferences with your committee, at your orals, and/or at professional poster sessions on research. Thus, the potential usefulness and importance of these displays suggests a need to dedicate time and care to creating them. Miles and Huberman (1994), among others, have provided excellent guidance in the development of visual displays of information. Once you have displayed your data visually, you are ready to start the challenging process of interpreting what each display means individually, and what the totality of your data mean. In addition, consider creating a figure or table which synthesizes your findings figuratively and/or literally.

Frequently doctoral students find that they "hop" between analyzing their data, and determining what their findings are. This process is particularly important for those who carry out hypothesis-generating research studies. As the researcher starts to make some generalizations from the data, moving towards a hypothesis, she or he will return to those data to seek confirmation of the emerging hypothesis. In this scenario, then, data analysis and interpretation are two sides of one coin, or reciprocal processes, each leading to the other.

It is your responsibility, from your in-depth familiarity with your data, to represent your data honestly and appropriately. The more support you can provide, the more likely your readers will be to concur with your analysis. Figure 12.1 graphically represents a cyclical process integral to the writing of your dissertation. Ultimately, there is a point at which you say, "Enough! I know what I've found." That's when you're ready to write the final draft of your findings.

Figure 12.1 *A schematic representation of the typical recursive process in writing a dissertation*

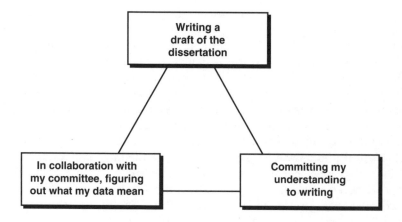

13 Presenting Your Findings
Drafting and Editing Your Dissertation

> Towards the completion of it all, it seemed that a new world had opened up to me. I found that exhilarating.

> The accomplishment of completing a rigorous academic effort is quite uplifting.

You are now ready to write up your findings in a polished state for public scrutiny. And "scrutiny" is the operative term. Expect that each of your "findings" will be subjected to intensive study. You will initially draft some organizational strategies projecting the potential contents of sections of your chapters. You will place in these sections all the relevant materials you have collected and analyzed. At first this will probably involve creating numerous files with scraps of papers, notes, transcripts, test scores, etc. Eventually, you will distill this amalgam of papers, identifying the most important issues and highlighting these in your presentation. You will constantly revise these as you proceed in presenting your findings. In actuality, you are probably discovering what you found concurrent with writing this section. Once a first draft is completed, you will be in a better position to revise your text, helping your readers to understand what you now know you have discovered.

Your chair may work with you in this process, or, more typically, will respond to drafts you provide. As you progress, you will get a better sense of where information should be presented to facilitate your readers' understanding of both the process and the outcomes of your study.

As agreed with your chair and your committee, you will offer drafts for their review. When you discuss their reactions and suggestions to your drafts, you should obtain clarity on confusing issues as well. There is usually a healthy intellectual dialog which occurs in this process during which time your analysis becomes enhanced, and your committee becomes informed of your progress directing and guiding your thinking. During these conversations, your committee may ask questions about your draft, to which you should be ready to respond. Look on these interactions as opportunities to explain what you have done, without being either defensive or docile. You should be able to explain your rationale, based on others who preceded you, or based on your understanding of the specific situation in which you found yourself. Regardless of the basis, be prepared to respond. If you believe your reader has misunderstood your meaning, be prepared to clarify your intent expansively and then revise your written text so that it is clearer for all subsequent readers. After you have taken a great deal of time thinking about issues, be prepared to defend your thinking while listening to alternative perspectives.

As the researcher, it is your responsibility to explain in great detail what you found: what you discovered from your data; what new insights you have about such phenomena as, for example, the way that people write essays in class or the way that books are organized. You serve as a guide to your readers, preventing them from getting lost looking at isolated trees, and helping them to see the forest the way that you now understand it, based on your intensive, careful analysis.

You will need to discover what you "found" before you can create the final textual presentation of this section. Most students find it useful to write many notes and drafts of this aspect of the research prior to polishing a chapter which reports on the findings. Consequently, students frequently create tables and figures, then explain what these syntheses of their data mean in narrative form, and, finally, organize these sections into a cohesive and powerful chapter of their dissertation which explains the findings.

Your data are the evidence supporting your findings. Based on your systematic and intensive interrogation of these data, you will infer potential explanations for them. Your inferences are data driven, based on your interpretation of what your data reveal. You may make some inferences which are not supported by your data. These you will need to discard. You want to identify inferences which both are supported by your data and *offer a comprehensive understanding of your data.*

As you obtain confidence in the fit between your data and the inference(s), you will explicitly state the inference(s) or *general principle(s)* which explain your findings. You may also want to identify any qualifications or limitations on those general principles, such as age, sex, or context.

This expansive presentation of your thinking will enable readers to follow your interpretation and ultimately accept your perspective when your explanation is reasonable to them. It will also enable you to review your thinking consciously, and perhaps find weaknesses or omissions which need to be remedied. If your interpretation is thorough, clear, logical, relevant, and cautious, it is likely to be compelling to your readers. And it will provide the opportunity for an informed discussion, along with an important contribution to your academic discipline.

Creating a Compelling Argument for your Findings

It is possible that your findings may contradict current thinking. If your findings "surprised" you in some way, and this is one important phenomenon inherent in the research process, then your findings are likely to surprise others. It is your responsibility to convince your readers at least to consider the accuracy of your analysis by providing sufficient information for them to make independent judgments. This may take the form of quotations from interviews, or test scores, for example. These samples of your data, in combination with your narrative explanation of the inferences you are making, will position your readers to consider your interpretation along with their own, weighing any differences, and particularly focusing on the elements which you emphasize in your presentation. There are several criteria which are useful in drafting a compelling argument:

a thorough interpretation;
a clear interpretation;
a logical interpretation;
a relevant interpretation;
a cautious interpretation.

A Thorough Interpretation

A thorough interpretation of your data *synthesizes* the individual units of analysis (e.g. words, sentences, responses, test scores, weight, etc.) into a more *comprehensive* context. For an interpretation to be considered "thorough," it needs to account for all the *major dimensions* which you studied, as identified in your research question. You will lead your readers to focus on the larger issues, a perspective which you have from your intimate familiarity with your data. Your ability to create a cohesive whole from the isolated bits and pieces of your data will be one factor in creating a thorough interpretation. Your explanations of the potential meanings to be drawn from data presented in spread sheets, figures, photos, excerpts from transcripts, etc., should be multi-dimensional, suggesting multiple potential perspectives on your data. As you guide your readers, you create a compelling argument for interpreting your data in a specific way. On the other hand, you may offer competing interpretations for your data. The choice you make is based on your data. If your data are clear cut, there is no controversy. In some cases, the data are not that clear cut, requiring an honest researcher to offer competing interpretations.

Your readers should have a sense that your interpretations represent an exhaustive search for meaning from your data. They should also get a sense that you have included all the essential information, and that you have not arbitrarily excluded information relevant to the analysis. Your honesty as a researcher is attested to by your comprehensive inclusion of all your data, even data which may challenge your inferences.

A Clear Interpretation

A clear interpretation is easy to follow. Information is presented systematically and predictably. Symbols in graphs and within the text are explained. Details are provided to enable an intelligent reader to understand the issues. There is meticulous attention to getting the facts correct. The information presented in a table should be consistent with the information presented in the narrative. When there are discrepancies, the reader is at a loss to know which is accurate, and therefore may become disillusioned with the quality of the research being reported. When transcripts are quoted, line references should be exact, directing your reader's attention to the precise words on which you are commenting. If a reader has difficulty following your argument, you jeopardize the possibility that your study will be misinterpreted or rejected. Your careful choice of words will reflect your clear understanding of your findings.

The organization of your information in a concise, flowing text evolves from a comprehensive and cohesive understanding of your findings, knowing which parts are subsumed under the key findings.

A Logical Interpretation

Your reader will consider your interpretation "logical" if you organize your presentation in a *systematic* and *predictable* fashion. From your understanding of your data, you decide which issue needs to be addressed first, and which follows naturally from that first issue. You will also provide a sketch of the order in which you will discuss your findings, enabling your readers to create a mental map of your presentation, and then to find that information as they peruse your text. Your presentation should lead your readers to understand your findings as clearly as you do. Usually, simultaneously with your writing of this section, your understanding becomes crystallized.

A Relevant Interpretation

Your findings must be directly related to three components of your study:

- your research question and the theories and/or sources which contributed to its identification;
- the data which you collected; and
- your data analysis.

Information from other sources is irrelevant at this point. Your interpretation must be focused on important issues. Whereas there may be many details included in the data which you collected, and your analysis may have focused on a multitude of elements, you now need to decide the *most important issues*. You want to highlight the most prominent, and the strongest findings that your study can provide. By diluting your presentation with numerous relatively trivial details, your major findings will be lost. While there may be a time when these relatively minor issues can be productively addressed, at this time it is important to address the major findings. Determining the "major" issues may be viewed as a judgment call. Certainly, as the person most familiar with your data and with your findings, you are considered to be in an ideal position to help us, your readers, to recognize and accept this focus. Thus, it becomes incumbent on you to help us see the light. Connect your findings with the major theories and research guiding *your* study.

A Cautious Interpretation

Some researchers make major pronouncements from their research, implying that they have solved all the questions in the world with their research. Others are timid about making any statements beyond the data which they collected. While these extremes are not unusual in first drafts of dissertations, doctoral students learn to make appropriately cautious interpretations.

A wise researcher takes care not to over-generalize from limited data. Being cautious, while making a case for what you *did* find, you will find an appropriate balance. Seeking critical readers' reactions to your analysis, you will have access to others' views on the match between your data and your proposed findings

Concluding Sections

Typically, doctoral studies conclude with at least one additional section in addition to an abstract of the study. These sections may be called "Summary," "Conclusions," "Implications," and/or "Recommendations." The need for details required in each section varies across institutions, so become familiar with the customs at your university and your chair's preferences.

Summary This usually includes a total recapitulation of all the elements of the study, including a statement of the problem, the research design, the findings, and the conclusions.

Conclusion This section makes assertions based on the findings. It usually addresses issues that support, or fail to support, a theory which is being tested. For example, if a hypothesis has been supported by the data, then the researcher may conclude that the data support the validity of the theory which was being tested in the study. Some researchers use the trends which were evident in their findings as a basis for potential theory building. This section states the researcher's sense of how the study's findings contribute to the knowledge in a discipline.

Implications In this section, the researcher is free to make a range of suggestions for the usefulness of the findings. The research settings may range from elementary grade classrooms, to university-based research projects; this is the researcher's opportunity to explain how the findings of the just-completed study may contribute to theories and/or practice in these settings. Another way of viewing this section is for the researcher to state the potential significance of the implications of the study on professional practice, or on life in general.

If you wrote a "Potential Significance" section for your dissertation proposal, you may return to that hypothetical section to reflect on the predictions you made. With the knowledge acquired from your findings, you may now revise these statements of potential significance to more accurately reflect your understanding of the possible impact of your study's findings.

Recommendations   You make recommendations based on your experiences in conducting the research as well as in any other professional capacity. You may recommend that other researchers (including future doctoral students) conduct additional studies in this area, which follow from the findings and procedures implemented in your study. While the liberty to speculate and tell others what to do is tantalizing, most doctoral students, and researchers generally, restrict their suggestions to a few targets. In actuality, many doctoral students follow up on their own studies, or advocate that students in their program continue with the same line of inquiry.

Abstract   Most institutions require you to write an abstract of your study. Often the abstract is the first part of your study which is read by your readers. It is frequently the only part read by others outside your institution. Create an abstract which clearly represents your study, focusing on the most significant elements. The information included in your abstract will influence whether researchers proceed to look at your total study. You will want people who are studying issues related to yours to find your study among all the others. You will also want your abstract to be an accurate representation of all the hard work you have devoted to this project. Most students find it useful initially to write an extended abstract, and then to pare down their words, so that the key issues are expressed concisely within the imposed limits.

An abstract of your study is usually published in *Dissertations Abstract International* (*DAI*). Although there is a 350-word restriction, the format is open to individual choice. The content typically includes the following:

- title;
- problem or issue which was researched;
- the frame of reference or theoretical bases which guided the study;
- the data sources which informed your study;
- the procedures for analyzing your data; and
- the outcomes or findings.

The number of words which you allot to each part will be unique to your abstract. Give great detail in reporting the more unusual parts of your study. Sometimes, in a desire to entice a reader to pursue the entire text, researchers provide sketchy information. Be cautious in writing your abstract, seek advice from your support group.

After numerous revisions, all these pieces of your dissertation are likely to be approved by your committee, led by your chair. They will decide that it is time to schedule orals. In most cases, this agreement reflects individual and collective concurrence that you have accomplished all that is required for approving the dissertation.

In rare instances, faculty agree to schedule orals despite the fact that they are not pleased with the dissertation. This may be precipitated by a student's resistance to committee members' suggestions. In such a situation, faculty may vote to fail the student at the oral examination. While most institutions offer the opportunity for a "second" oral defense, students want to avoid this situation, if at all possible. For most doctoral candidates, the scheduling of orals reflects a major accomplishment, and is prelude to a celebration of their work: "When my mentor finally said, 'You can defend,' I felt the Glory come upon me!"

14 Defending Your Dissertation
Preparing for Orals

I'm excited to talk about my study, now that it's done!

I sat at orals with people who had been my teachers and finally saw myself as a quasi-peer.

When you've decided, "I've done the best I can do," there is one more step in the completion of your dissertation. You have probably heard it referred to in some of these ways:

- orals;
- your orals;
- the defense;
- your defense;
- a hearing;
- your hearing;
- an oral examination.

Your institutions terms may reveal important insights. If we look more closely at the names, we will note subtle potential differences in the focus of this culminating experience. For example, when candidates prepare for a "defense" they are typically placed in a position which is different from "orals." As a candidate at a "defense" you are likely to be asked to defend the theories, stances, and decisions which you made in the process of writing your dissertation. You are more likely to experience a confrontation, a time when there is a need to "defend" what was done and why it was done. At a session labeled "orals" the candidate may consider and speculate about multiple perspectives on theories and other issues, without necessarily defending one stance. The use of the term "your" makes your orals more personal. Certainly each person's experience is unique, never to be duplicated precisely by any other candidate. Regardless of the name it is given at your institution, there are two interdependent processes which occur:

- you publicly discuss what you researched, why you studied it, what you discovered in the process, and how your study contributes to the scholarship in your area of specialization, while

- your committee makes an academic evaluation about the adequacy of your dissertation and your oral presentation.

Since I think most institutions use this event as a time to hear from the candidate in an academic setting, I will use the term "oral" and the plural term "orals" in this discussion. (As in all aspects of the dissertation process, I strongly urge you to inquire about what happens at this event from your committee and from your collegial support group. These people have the most intimate details to offer which should be useful in your preparation for this important day, a most-memorable day in your academic career.)

In the main, orals are a positive experience, a time when the candidate gets to talk extensively about all she or he has learned and the enduring questions which may guide future research: "Dr. L told me that the orals were to be a happy occasion and not one to grill and intimidate the person." Smith notes:

> Much will depend on the quality of research done, the kind of rapport one has with the committee, and the amount of ego strength that one has at the end of this whole process. For some students it is agony. The committee may be rough and the student may be very anxious. These students go in thinking that the committee will try to trick them. In essence, they have set the tone for their own defense.
>
> Other students may experience complete ecstasy because they feel that writing the dissertation is one of the most creative things they have ever done. These students usually feel good about what they have done, and they go in with the attitude that they know more about their dissertation than anyone else does. They enter with a willingness to share this knowledge.
>
> Reactions to the defense are as varied as the defense itself. Some students end up with ambivalent feelings; others are so relieved to have finished that they do not know exactly how to feel. Many students are simply happy because the defense has gone very well for them. Although the feelings may be different, no one will deny that a real sense of accomplishment is there. No one can destroy that.
>
> (Smith, 1982, p. 43)

The Purpose

Academic institutions constantly evaluate. For you to gain admission into your doctoral program, your academic record was scrutinized. During all your courses, your work was evaluated. Prior to writing your dissertation, your proposal was subjected to careful review. And now that the individual members of your committee have each decided that your dissertation is ready for orals, they will evaluate your work publicly. There are basically four purposes accomplished by your orals:

- quality control;
- academic conversation among peers;
- dissemination; and
- closure.

Each institution is concerned with sustaining an implicit academic standard. Your dissertation will be revised to insure that it meets the university's standard for acceptable scholarship. The oral defense is one setting where that quality control is evidenced. It is not one faculty member's judgment, but rather a collective decision which yields a "pass" on your oral examination.

The orals provide the opportunity for an academic conversation among peers. Now that you have completed a rigorous research project, your research apprenticeship is ending. Your orals mark this transition as you are invited to sit at the table and talk about your research as a peer with your professors. The professors are initially evaluating and ultimately acknowledging that you have met the criteria for membership in the community of research scholars. Your ideas are as highly valued as theirs, and you have an equal place at the table.

Another objective of the orals is to disseminate the findings of your study. Your orals are the first time you will talk formally about your dissertation's findings. This event is important in the academic world. You are sharing valuable information on new scholarship which has the potential to contribute to the advancement of knowledge in a specific discipline, probably the discipline in which your committee members are respected experts. With your knowledge from your just completed research study, you are now expected to provide authoritative insight into previously uncharted or contested issues.

Following your isolation and immersion in your research, you will want to disseminate your findings to others who are part of your new community. By sharing your findings you enable others to have access to "cutting edge" information, the Holy Grail of most academics. This is also the opportunity for you to rehearse how you may present your study in other academic settings, such as at job interviews, graduate seminars, and professional conferences. You are the key informant at the orals. You are an expert, more knowledgeable about the specific area you studied than anyone else at the table (and ideally anyone else in the international academic community as well). You should be well-prepared to present information persuasively and articulately.

This is also the time to bring closure on your doctoral program and to celebrate your enhanced knowledge and expertise. You have devoted an extensive amount of time and energy to this, and your orals are a time for marking the end of this endeavor, a time to move on to new projects.

The Players

Participants at your orals may be restricted to your committee. Alternatively, the occasion may extend to the wider academic community, even reaching out to experts at distant universities. There may be an opportunity for students who are "in the pipeline" and expecting to have their orals in the near future to attend. You may even invite some friends and family members. The university may assign additional faculty from related disciplines who become "outside readers," providing perspectives not present among your committee. The university wants to provide you with a fair opportunity to present your research while insuring that their standards are being maintained. Each institution creates a process for operationalizing these concerns. It is most often the case that there is at least one academic participant at your orals who was not a committee member. These persons may have independent votes on your dissertation or they may be considered advisors to the original committee.

The committee members are usually happy to see you at this point in the process, and want to make the experience pleasurable as well as intellectually memorable. The external readers, however, frequently see themselves in a different position. They consider themselves the final gate-keepers, striving to validate the candidate's expertise through rigorous inquiry. Since they typically have little or no history with the candidate, their introduction to you is through your dissertation. They use your document exclusively to focus their questions at your orals. They may want to learn more about a process which is new to them, or they may want to inquire about a controversial issue. It is your responsibility to convince them that you are knowledgeable, but not all-knowing; that you have learned a great deal, but that your learning continues. Your inquiring mind will function after the orals, and you may want to follow up on some issues which emerge at this event.

The purpose of the expanded committee is manifold:

- Your committee, recognizing that their work will be reviewed by others in their field, will establish rigorous standards in their evaluation of your work.
- The institution's reputation will be enhanced by the approval of graduates' dissertations by acknowledged experts in the discipline.
- The student will be protected from personal tensions which may have developed among the established committee members and the candidate.

You are typically notified of the names of all the individuals who will serve on your orals. You will want to "check out" information about the external readers, those who are new to the conversation on your dissertation. Find out what they've written, what their areas of expertise are, and what their predispositions are on controversial issues in your specialization. Ask about them in your peer support group. This information will assist you in your preparation. In most cases, outside readers ask important questions, but rarely disagree with the committee on their final evaluation. Your committee is typically more numerous than the outsiders, frequently of higher rank, and certainly more knowledgeable about the dissertation itself. On the other hand, there are times when the external readers take the opportunity at least to make it difficult for the candidate to achieve a "pass." For example, you may find that a person whom you initially excluded from your committee has now been assigned as an external reader. You will need to acknowledge that individual's expertise as an evaluator of your dissertation. You may need to make an exceptionally impressive presentation to win this person over to your side, to accept your dissertation at least as "satisfactory."

Lee found that his two external readers came from a department with a philosophy which was the antithesis of his own and that of his committee. On applying for a doctoral program, Lee intentionally eliminated the program which they directed from consideration because its philosophy was different from his own. How amazed he was when he discovered that they would be final arbiters on his dissertation! Since the selection of external readers is typically not open to negotiation, he was stuck with these two. He worried about the conflict, and conferred with his chair about the potential problem. His chair assured him that all would be "OK. This is an academic exercise; they will have their say, but they can't stop you from having your say." Unfortunately, Lee's premonitions were realized. The two external readers engaged in a personal attack on Lee and his ideas, never addressing any academic issues. Ultimately, they, in tandem, threw copies of his dissertation on the floor. He will never forget that episode. Nor will his committee. Lee's dissertation "passed," but he has scars that will never heal (as do the faculty and the institution).

Cassandra is still reeling from her experience. As she was writing her dissertation, she found she was in constant conflict with her chair. Ultimately, she decided that she would need to change chairs if she was ever going to get done. She sought the assistance of another professor in the same department, who reluctantly agreed to take on the role of chair. As Cassandra continued with her writing, she realized there was little enthusiasm from her new chair. Cassandra finally got to a point where she believed she was done, and asked her chair to schedule orals. Her chair did so, half-heartedly. When the external reviewers were appointed, the dispossessed chair was named as one of the readers. Cassandra knew she was not in an enviable position. Her chair was not a great advocate, and one of the external readers was clearly opposed to her work, and probably personally distressed with the way she had treated him. At the orals, she found considerable dissension, even from her chair. To Cassandra's amazement, she was required to make major changes in her dissertation prior to rescheduling a second orals. Cassandra believed that everyone gets through – and that's partly why she pushed so hard. She had no idea that the faculty might turn her work down, especially after she had devoted so much time to this project. At the time of this writing, Cassandra has yet to complete a second document to present to her chair, finding herself "blocked" in her writing and diverted by other activities.

Despite these two horror stories, most candidates make it through their orals. In fact these stories are so powerful in part because they are so unusual. But passing orals may not be the end. Frequently it is recommended that changes are made to the final document, but the orals themselves are usually completed with the understanding that when the recommended changes are accomplished, the dissertation will be accepted.

In some respects the orals may seem anticlimactic. You typically have received the approval of your committee. You may have already passed the "format" review. It all seems to be done. But, as we all know, "it's not over till it's signed on the dotted line." So, do not become smug. This is serious business, with fragile egos, and unpredictable players. You will need to display a level of authority along with respect for the knowledge of all your reviewers. At the orals you have the opportunity and the need to perform as a scholar representing the rigorous study which you conducted. All you have done has prepared you for this moment. You need to provide elaborate explanations on all your work, offering great details on all your decision-making, and all your major findings.

Vartuli tells us:

> As with the dissertation-writing process, the oral defense of the dissertation can be a rewarding or defeating experience depending on the feedback students receive concerning their work. If graduate students lack feedback, they tend to feel more nervous, insecure, and defensive. [Then, quoting from one of her informants:]
>
> I didn't like the oral defense of my dissertation. I really didn't. I had worked myself up into a real snit about that because I hadn't gotten enough feedback from my adviser about the dissertation. He wrote me a one-page letter saying that it ranged from inspired to pedantic. I was sure that most of it was pedantic and very little of it was inspired.

After investing so much time and energy in a project, students find that the dissertation becomes an extension of themselves. Some see the oral defense as defending who they are. [Quoting from another informant:]

> When in generals I was just defending ideas ... all the ideas in the dissertation were mine: from what was included, how it was done, to the arrangement of the research design. I felt very personally threatened by any kind of criticism of any of that. I think if I went into it again now, I wouldn't feel that way about it. I've distanced myself enough from it that now I don't take the criticism personally.

Personal pressures also hinder feelings of self-worth at this stage. If the student feels her own expectations are not met, then the process holds less satisfaction.

> Graduate students receiving positive feedback on their dissertations tend to go into the oral defense confident and secure. The experience can actually be "fun." She is the expert, and a discussion of her work with colleagues is quite an ego boost.
>
> (Vartuli, 1982, p. 11)

The Process

The orals are a fairly formal event, often with written invitations to the entire academic community (although typically few take the time to participate beyond the members of your committee). There is usually a prescribed amount of time dedicated to the orals, typically a two-hour time block in a room away from the hustle of daily pressures, perhaps even a room dedicated to orals. The standard arrangement is a seminar table with the doctoral candidate surrounded by the hearing committee. Typically each faculty member arrives with a copy of your dissertation in hand. They have each had time to read your document carefully, and are prepared for an intense, academic discussion uninterrupted by phone calls or drop-in conversations. Each faculty member expects to have an opportunity to ask you questions and to listen to the responses you provide to the others at your orals. They dedicate their total attention to you at the time of your orals. They anticipate a lively intellectual interchange.

You are clearly in the hot seat – although this is your day, it is the time to perform. You need to be assertive about your knowledge, clearly in command of all that you did and of the professional literature which informs your understanding. You need to display confidence in your knowledge and offer expansive responses to questions and issues on the table. From your committee, expect to hear questions similar to ones which they posed as you went through the entire project. You may ask them if there's anything they'd like you to prepare. Certainly ask them what to expect. All this information will be important. There are some predictable questions.

Typical questions at orals

- What were your findings?
- What surprised you?
- What would you do differently?
- Why did you do A instead of B?
- What motivated you to do *this* study?
- Who are the major theorists who influenced your thinking?
- What are the conflicts in the field?
- What studies most contributed to your understanding of the issues?
- In what ways will your work contribute to knowledge in your specialization?
- In what ways will your work contribute to clarifying the conflicts in your field?
- Please explain Figure X.
- Are you familiar with X's work at Y University on this very topic?
- Where do you think your specialization is going now?
- If you were starting today to create a research project, what might it be? Might it build on your own study?
- If you were asked to participate in reconceptualizing our doctoral program, what might you suggest we consider?

You can prepare for your orals by responding to these questions, explaining in great detail the evolution of your thinking. Writing notes to bring with you on the day of your orals may be useful. Certainly, you are free to refer to your dissertation as you respond to questions which are posed. Many students place color-coded tabs at key points in the dissertation to facilitate access to specific issues.

Some remember the questions posed as being "picky." For one candidate the comment that a particular researcher's work was not mentioned "got my dukes up. I couldn't understand why that was so important." If that happens to you, try to consider what you know about that researcher's work and connect it with yours, offering that you could/should have included the name and will! If, on the other hand, you are unfamiliar with the person's work, acknowledge this and inquire about the connection to your own work. (You're not expected to be all-knowing. In fact, admitting that you do not know everything is considered an appropriate stance.)

The oral is not totally focused on the candidate, although most candidates assume this to be the case. Rather, orals are a unique time in the academic calendar when professors come together to talk with faculty colleagues about scholarly matters. This coming together contrasts with the virtual isolation of faculty with their students during the major portion of the academic year. For some faculty this is a cherished opportunity to talk with peers about important scholarly matters, trying, for example, to understand evolving paradigms or new perspectives in their discipline. For others, a student's orals offers an opportunity to "get back" at a faculty colleague in a public forum for some perceived professional or personal offense, or long-standing competition or jealousy.

To move beyond any personal disputes, candidates explain in elaborate detail their understanding of the issues which are addressed. They acknowledge conflicts in the field (every field has conflicts!) and carefully present their reasoning for advancing one position over another. It would be prudent to acknowledge your biases and the bases for these, while recognizing the possibility of other perspectives on the same issue. Avoid polemics; try to accommodate a wide range of perspectives. You know this is probably the final hurdle in the process. Being successful at your orals will be based on your knowledge and diplomacy.

At your orals you can expect a fairly formal structure. On the day of your orals, the person who will chair them informs you of the procedures to be followed. You will probably be asked to start the conversation, providing an overview of the issue you researched, why you researched it, how you went about conducting your research, and what your findings were. Some students prepare overhead transparencies or a PowerPoint presentation of an initial "overview" of the study, finding it easier to face the screen than the faces of the inquirers at the start. (If this is comfortable for you and acceptable at your university, you may need to assure yourself that the appropriate equipment will be available.)

At the oral defense I was asked both technical and theoretical questions. After the congratulations were offered me, the conversation took a different quality. Different, more in-depth questions were asked of me. It seemed as if the door had opened and I moved into the room of professionals and was accepted as belonging to the club. That was memorable and disturbing.

After the questioning ends, the candidate is asked to leave the room temporarily for the committee "to decide." Typically each professor present at your orals has the opportunity and responsibility to vote on whether or not you "pass." In most instances, the candidate needs to obtain positive votes from a majority of those participating. The faculty individually complete forms in which they record a grade of "pass," or "re-do," or "fail." They then collectively discuss changes, if any, they will require before the dissertation is officially accepted by the university. After what seems like a long time, but usually is only about five minutes, they invite the candidate to return to the room and share their collective decision. It is not unusual for a successful candidate to be invited back into the room, and reintroduced to the orals committee as Dr. —! At this point there is much congratulating: the committee congratulates the student, the student offers thanks to the committee, and then they each go on to other things.

The Outcome

Each faculty member votes on whether or not the candidate has successfully completed the orals. In most cases, the vote is predictable: there is at least a majority, if not a unanimous vote to approve. There may also be requests for clarification, revision, or expansion of the text. Usually, the dissertation chair is charged with insuring that these requests are addressed in the finally approved document.

In the rare case where there are a majority of negative votes, several different recommendations may be made. For example:

* redo the dissertation and reschedule orals;
* schedule a second orals;
* or terminate matriculation.

These are unusual, but they do happen. Many people who have received these evaluations complete their degrees, either at this institution or at another place. But, in the main, most people who have their orals, graduate from that institution. The chances are good that if you have taken the time to read this book, and to understand the apprenticeship process, you will succeed and complete your dissertation.

Once you have completed your dissertation, three feelings are generally experienced: exhilaration, exhaustion, and dejection. Finally getting to the end of the trail, you get a feeling of accomplishment. Your tension exhausts you, and then you feel alone. All those who had been concerned about getting you to this point may have no further role in your life: "There was no champagne toast after the defense. There was nothing. The committee congratulated me and rushed off to another event." Some relate this last let-down to post-partum depression. To avoid this, many doctoral students contemplate their lives-after-dissertation while preparing for orals, if not before. They make plans to get involved in new projects immediately after the orals, particularly those they deferred while working on the dissertation.

At some institutions there is a ritual "sherry-sharing" time following the orals, which helps to ease the experience. As the faculty and new doctor sip sherry, they discuss new projects, and issues such as publication of the dissertation and finding new employment. Oftentimes, the new doctor continues working with some of the committee members transforming her or his dissertation into a journal article. Clearly the respect which all the members develop for each other's work makes the prospect of continued collaboration very attractive.

Once you get to this point, you have three essential responsibilities:

1 Honor those who supported your progress
2 Help others to succeed and
3 Promote the reconceptualization of the entire dissertation process.

Good luck!

Appendix A

Doctoral Students' Experiences: Expectations of Doctoral Studies[1]

Although doctoral programs and doctoral recipients implicitly value research, there is little systematic investigation on the effects of the doctoral process on those who participate. To address this issue, in part, this study focused on one specific aspect: the expectations of doctoral students. The objective of the research was to obtain the participants' perspectives on their experiences as these connected with their expectations. University *Bulletins* give little or no explanation of what enrollment in a doctoral program entails.

I sought assistance in understanding a process which has been seemingly "cloaked in darkness and secrecy." By studying and reflecting on the expectations of doctoral students, we can, as professionals, ascertain the match between our students' expectations and the activities we require in the process of completing a doctoral program. Participants in the study were either currently enrolled or previously enrolled in doctoral programs across the USA, leading to either EdD or PhD degrees.

Theoretical Perspective

Several perspectives informed this study. One issue was the large number of students who "drop out" of doctoral programs (Lovitts, 1996). Although numbers are difficult to obtain, with clear differences across universities and programs within each university, the generally agreed number is 50 per cent. At universities where doctoral students are funded for their programs, enrolled as full-time, residential students, the graduation rate is significantly higher than at universities where students' personal savings are the basis for their tuition, and where students frequently enroll as part-time, commuter students. Bowen and Rudenstine's (1992) study, *In Pursuit of the PhD*, documents that:

> The percentage of students [in Arts and Sciences programs in selected American universities] who never earn PhDs, in spite of having achieved ABD status, has risen in both larger and smaller programs. ... The direction of change is unmistakable, and the absolute numbers are high enough to be grounds for serious concern.
>
> (Bowen and Rudenstine, 1992, p. 253)

A related issue is whether the number of students who do not complete their programs is higher for female participants than for their male counterparts. This issue is a potential concern since we know that doctoral students in education programs are more likely to be female. Holland and Eisenhart (1990), for example, provide important perspectives on the social pressures facing women's academic achievements which may affect their commitment to complete an academic program. While Holland and Eisenhart were studying undergraduate women, the issues are similar, and perhaps even more intense for women pursuing advanced degrees.

Faculty in academic institutions need to know the participants' perspectives of what is expected and experienced in the process of acquiring the doctoral degree. Ted Sizer (1997), a leader in education reform, recently commented on the frequency with which doctoral students wisely drop out of doctoral programs. He believes this is due to the realization that the program routinely requires a "retrogressive model of inquiry" which is so alien to the students' inductive and interactive methods of inquiry that they find no value in going through the process. Clearly he has offered us a challenge that we dismiss at our peril. Lovitts (1996) and Vartuli (1982) documented the disjuncture many participants find between academic programs and their real-world experiences and needs.

In addition to addressing concerns within the academy, there has been a call from the public at large to study the PhD process, as evidenced by a recent article in *The New York Times Magazine* (Menand, 1996). There is clearly a concern for the autonomy of doctoral programs which show no evidence of accountability to the profession or the students who enroll. The purpose of this study is to provide some baseline data to understand the expectations of students who enroll in doctoral programs.

Modes of Inquiry

Open-ended questionnaires were mailed to graduates of doctoral programs, requesting their typewritten, anonymous responses as well as their distribution of the questionnaire to others holding the doctoral degree, those pursuing the doctoral degree, and known ABDs. Included with the instructions for responding to this questionnaire was an invitation to participate in informal roundtable discussions or conversations. In addition, faculty members at a wide array of institutions distributed questionnaires in their doctoral courses and to colleagues, enlarging the data pool.

The researcher received written responses to the open-ended questionnaires and responses of individuals interested in participating in the roundtable discussions. Three small roundtable discussions, each of approximately three hours' duration, and ten one-hour interviews provided additional data for this inquiry.

The data include written responses to the open-ended questionnaire and transcribed tapes from the roundtable discussions and interviews. In all, close to 200 individuals responded to the open-ended written questionnaires, and fifteen people participated in the informal three-hour roundtable discussions and the ten one-hour interviews. While responses were received from across the nation, the researcher acknowledges that the volunteers who took the time to respond to the questionnaire or participate in the discussions may not have been representative of the total pool of doctoral participants. But the number of individuals who made the time to respond to these issues does suggest a need to consider their responses carefully. This is particularly true since there were so many common threads among the responses of people who attended different doctoral programs.

Findings

What started out as a seemingly simple question has become increasingly complex. There seem to be two major reasons people enter into a doctoral program: intrinsic reward and extrinsic reward. Those who are seeking some intrinsic reward are enrolling for their own, personal fulfillment and enrichment. Those who are seeking an extrinsic reward, are fulfilling an externally imposed requirement, often from professional institutions. Using these two categories, we can create three different groups of students. These three groups are represented in Figure A.1.

One group (Group A) identified exclusively *intrinsic, personal reasons* for pursuing the degree:

• I wanted to do something for myself.
• I wanted to learn more.

Figure A.1   *Student expectations on entering doctoral programs*

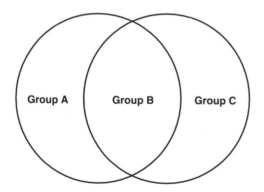

Note
Group A = those seeking personal enrichment, those with intrinsic motivation
Group B = those with both intrinsic and extrinsic motivation (personal enrichment and external pressures)
Group C = those with extrinsic motivation, responding to external pressures

A second group (Group B) identified a *combination of intrinsic (personal reasons) and extrinsic (external mandates) rewards*:

- I wanted to get a PhD; I wanted to teach at a college.
- I wanted to change my career. I wanted to see if I could get a PhD; I wanted to learn more. My husband encouraged me to go.

A third group (Group C) identified exclusively fulfilling an *extrinsic reward, accommodating others' requirements*:

- I needed the doctorate to keep my job which I really liked at X University.
- I realized that people with the degree were listened to; those without it were not.

Same Phenomenon – Different Perspectives

Many of the participants viewed experiences as obstacles; others perceived these same experiences as a way to grow in different ways: for example, to become more independent, more knowledgeable, more confident. Different motivations may have influenced their views of their experiences.

Some participants provided striking metaphors for the process: Many referred to the process as one of "going through hoops." One participant presented this quite forcefully:

> I think what you learn about jumping through hoops to finish is probably, in the long run, more valuable than the academic lessons that you learn as you went through the process. ... I think the hoop piece stays with you more. It's a better reason to hire someone with a doctorate than what they know.

One thought of the process as "going up a huge mountain," while another connected it to a "coming of age experience." In a recent article by Fahrenthold (1997), in the *Harvard Crimson*, Steven Ozment, a professor of ancient and modern history at Harvard was quoted as saying, "I worked day and night on that dissertation. It was the most horrible experience I think I've ever had" (p. 3).

The perceptions were all personal, focusing on a few significant themes. The *positive* experiences included the following:

Feeling creative, smart, and self-confident

- exhilaration while gathering data and analyzing it;
- pride at recognizing writing and other proficiencies ("I have good organization and integration skills");

- pride from presenting at conferences and publishing in professional journals ("I can do anything!"; "I figured it was all right for me to speak up and say what I wanted to say");
- confidence that they were respected as more knowledgeable in their professional posts as evidenced by appointments to tenure track university-based faculty lines and/or school district administrator responsibilities.

Expanding group of friends

- support groups reduced the alienation and isolation which surfaced at specific, crucial stages in the process;
- enjoyment of having a group of friends whom they saw at professional conferences.

Understanding one's learning process, including persevering despite adversity

- pleasure at identifying and achieving a goal – an intellectual goal and pursuit;
- a desire to continue learning – even enrolling in additional graduate programs;
- "it was a wonderful intellectual journey .... very intellectually challenging;"
- "I figured out that all this has to do with people and how people get along – and how you need to deal with people to make this thing go along – and how you can derail yourself from succeeding for reasons that have zero to do with the academic piece. I had a career in politics afterwards";
- being resolute in completing the challenge of getting the degree, "I've come this far, I'm not leaving empty-handed."

The *negative* experiences included:

Feeling resentment and fear

- "I didn't expect it to take up my life the way it did!"; "I can only give up this amount of time and spend it on myself and my dissertation and whatever, because I have this family that needs me";
- "I never needed anyone's help to do something like this before. I kind of resent that";
- dissertation seminar was a frequent setting for feeling resentment. Common comments were: "It was the worst!" "We needed to support each other – or else there was nothing." "It was a waste of time!" "I feared going there each week – but feared more what would happen if I didn't go!"

- some commented on how their mentor "protected" them – helping them to avoid attending dissertation seminar;

Feeling totally isolated and unprepared for writing the dissertation

- feeling dependent at a time when independence was assumed – remarking particularly at having so little information about what to expect in the process, how to conduct the research, and how to write it up – how to get it all together;
- unprepared for the need to obtain permission and approval for activities in the dissertation, one student remarked, "I thought it was *my* project;"
- not realizing how much input and collaboration was required with the faculty committee. In desperation, asking, "What do you [my major professor] want me to do?";
- "I had a very romantic idea – I thought I'd be flying to England and going into a library with dark panelling – and I thought I'd be discovering some brand new thing about language and thinking. ... It's the incremental steps that I was not prepared for when I was imagining what the dissertation process would be like. I saw it in a gestalt – kind of a whole – an enlighten-ment, and I didn't realize the intricate, detailed work that has to go into it – the revision and rethinking in my case";
- having conflicting feelings "being told that you are becoming the expert in a field – and not feeling comfortable with that – and yet they [your committee] still challenges you even though you are supposed to be the new authority";
- "needing to rely on others – yet not having comfortable access to this community";
- "anyone who has *not* gone through this process could not possibly under-stand what we're going through – no one in my family could believe what I'm doing!";
- distress at recognizing the need for external pressure to keep working;
- dismay at negative responses to drafts of the dissertation proposal;
- "I was always told what to do – you were always out to please Prof. X."

Feeling shell-shocked when done

- experiencing so many extreme emotions in very brief timespans;
- needing time to put everything into perspective;
- not being ready to talk about it;
- trying to figure out what really happened.

Synthesis

When there are conflicts between the expectations and the experiences of the participants, there is a need both to acknowledge and remedy the situation. The one constant theme, whether perceived as a positive or negative experience, was the lack of knowledge. Some saw this lack of knowledge as an asset, suggesting that if they had known what was involved in the process, they would probably never have started. But they quickly added that they believed they would have regretted that. There was a clear desire to know as much as possible about the process so that they could predict what was going to happen, allocate time and money wisely, and understand their roles in that process. One individual noted that the lack of any information about the length of time the program would take and when to expect to be done became unsettling for her/him, fearful that "the money would run out before finally completing the dissertation." Explicit information, respondents believed, would make it easier to manage their responsibilities within and beyond their doctoral program, as well as enabling them to feel more knowledgeable about their progress. Without this information, they felt very vulnerable, as they were totally dependent on others, particularly their committee.

Many students believe the dissertation is an extended examination in which they must independently display their acquired knowledge. When they encounter a dissertation director who expects them to consider the dissertation as a transformative learning experience, with an apprenticeship of sorts, they are astounded – unprepared for such an experience.

Many of the individuals compare their experiences to others'. Most believe "I didn't have as many upsets as I've heard other people have." Many can relate at least one "horror story," which at the time they were involved in the process was perceived as traumatic. These events ranged from the death of a mentor to the disappearance of the only copy of a chapter. For some this was the reason for dropping out, but most who had experienced such an event had completed the process and saw the "upset" as a challenge to surmount.

Emergent Hypotheses

Several hypotheses are displayed in Table A.1. There were three different motivations which brought people to doctoral programs. I have classified these as: *extrinsic* (professional requirement), *intrinsic* (personal enrichment), or a *combination* of professional extrinsic and intrinsic rewards. Typically, those who were accommodating professional requirements (the extrinsic reward group) held a view that the process of completing a dissertation involved a considerable amount of hazing, jumping through hoops, and documenting their current knowledge. In contrast, those who were pursuing a doctoral degree for intrinsic purposes expected to have a transformative experience, to learn and grow personally in the process. The third group believed that there would be both elements in the process (some hoop jumping, along with a personal transformation).

With time, these motivations and expectations frequently changed. For

Table A.1 Doctoral students' experiences: expectations and realizations

Expectations	Initial expectations			Ultimate experiences		
Rewards:	Extrinsic	Intrinsic	Combination	Extrinsic	Intrinsic	Combination
Experiences:	Hoops	Enrich	Hoops & enrich	Hoops	Enrich	Hoops & enrich
Extrinsic						
Group 1	✔			✔		
Group 2	✔					✔
Group 3	✔				✔	
Intrinsic						
Group 4		✔			✔	
Group 5		✔		✔		
Group 6		✔				✔
Combination						
Group 7			✔			✔
Group 8			✔	✔		
Group 9			✔		✔	

example, those identified in Groups 1–3 all entered with a similar expectation – that there were extrinsic rewards which would be accomplished by jumping through hoops. Many, but not all, changed their minds in the process: Group 1 identifies those whose views were unchanged; Group 2 expanded their view, including a combination of both hoop jumping and personal enrichment; Group 3, on the other hand, placed most of their focus ultimately on their personal enrichment, having changed their minds totally about the experience.

We see similar changes in the other two initial stances. Groups 4–6 all entered with intrinsic expectations, seeking to do the dissertation for themselves, to enhance their minds. With time, some of their views changed. Group 4 remained the same. Group 5 later came to believe the process was merely one of jumping through hoops, and not the intellectual journey they expected. Others (Group 6) expanded their concept, incorporating a combination of personal fulfillment along with jumping through hoops.

Groups 7–9 started with the expectation that the dissertation would require a combination of some hoop jumping along with some personally fulfilling experiences. Some continued to hold that view through the process. Others, however, became convinced that the process was mainly focused on the hoop jumping, while others still were totally immersed in enriching their minds and their lives.

Ultimately, some may believe that they are becoming informed about and proficient at important aspects of their professional responsibilities concurrent with the writing of their dissertation. Some may believe that it was exclusively a professional requirement, a set of hoops needing to be jumped. For some these are mutually exclusive perceptions, while, for the large majority, the combination seems to represent their reality.

While I did not initially attempt to distinguish between recent and more established recipients of the degree, as I conducted one of the roundtable discussions, I noticed a distinct difference between these two groups. Those early in the process seem almost clueless as to what the writing of a dissertation entails – comparing it to a long paper – while those who are in the process of writing the proposal or the dissertation seem most articulate in their expression of negative feelings. These are somewhat counterbalanced by those for whom at least four years have elapsed since graduation. The comments from this latter group were much more universally positive, recognizing that in the process of completing their programs, they became more confident learners with new perspectives on their worlds.

Implications

Doctoral programs need to understand the confusions of their students, and help students to understand the "method in the madness." This would reduce the drop-out rate. Another issue is aligning programs with participants' needs and expectations, or perhaps selecting students for programs with similar values and expectations. If we want to help students complete the programs they are enrolled in, we need to create structures which will help this to happen.

There was a general feeling of appreciation among respondents at being asked about their feelings. Participants were happy to know someone cared about and valued their feelings. Remarkably perhaps, their experiences still resonated with them – as if the experience was a recent one – despite the fact that some had graduated more than twenty-five years ago. As responsible educators, I think we need to consider these data as suggestive of some issues to discuss in our home settings – and perhaps on a broader scale – to open up the discussion of what the degree is intended to accomplish. I look forward to participating in such discussions.

Notes

1 Based on a paper originally presented at the Eastern Educational Research Association, February, 1997, Hilton Head Island, SC.

Appendix B
Suggested Reading on the Doctoral Dissertation

Anzul, M.E. (n.d.) *On writing a dissertation proposal*, Madison, NJ: Quest Associates.

Becker, H.S. (1986) *Writing for social scientists: How to start and finish your thesis, book, or article*, Chicago: University of Chicago Press.

Bolker, J. (1998) *Writing your dissertation in fifteen minutes a day: A guide to starting, revising, and finishing your doctoral thesis*, New York: Henry Holt and Company.

Cone, J.D. and Foster, S.L. (1993) *Dissertation and theses from start to finish: Psychology and related fields*, Washington, DC: American Psychological Association.

Delamont, S., Atkinson, P. and Parry, O. (1997) *Supervising the PhD: A guide to success*, Philadelphia: Open University Press.

Glatthorn, A.A. (1998) *Writing the winning dissertation: A step-by-step guide*, Thousand Oaks, CA: Corwin Press.

Goodchild, L.F., Green, K.E., Katz, E.L. and Kluever, R.C. (eds.) (1997) "Rethinking the dissertation process: Tackling personal and institutional obstacles," *New Directions for Higher Education*, 99, 25(3).

Hawley, P. (1993) *Being bright is not enough: The unwritten rules of doctoral study*, New York: Charles C. Thomas.

Locke, L., Spirduso, W.W. and Silverman, S.J. (1987) *Proposals that work: A guide for planning dissertations and grant proposals*, second edition, Thousand Oaks, CA: Sage.

Meloy, J.M. (1994) *Writing the qualitative dissertation*, Hillsdale, NJ: Erlbaum Associates.

Ogden, E.H. (1993) *Completing your doctoral dissertation or master's thesis in two semesters or less*, second edition. Lancaster, PA: Technomic Publishing.

Phillips, E.M. and Pugh, D.S. (1987) *How to get a PhD: A handbook for students and their supervisors*, second edition, Philadelphia: Open University Press.

Rossman, M.H. (1995) *Negotiating graduate school: A guide for graduate students*, Thousand Oaks, CA: Sage.

Sternberg, D. (1981) *How to complete and survive a doctoral dissertation*, New York: St. Martin's Press.

Appendix C
Suggested Reading on the Academic World

Blaxter, L., Hughes, C. and Tight, M. (1998) *The academic career handbook*, Philadelphia: Open University Press.

Bowen, W.G. and Rudenstine, N.L. (1992) *In pursuit of the PhD*, Princeton, NJ: Princeton University Press.

Clark, B.R. (1987) *The academic life: Small worlds, different worlds*, Princeton, NJ: Carnegie Foundation for the Advancement of Teaching.

Delamont, S., Atkinson, P. and Parry, O. (1997) *Supervising the Ph.D.: A guide to success*, Philadelphia: Open University Press.

Goodchild, L.F., Green, K.E., Katz, E.L. and Kluever, R.C. (eds.) (1997) Rethinking the dissertation process: Tackling personal and institutional obstacles. *New Directions for Higher Education*, 99, 25(3).

Heureux, J.L. (1996) *The handmaid of desire*, New York: Soho Press.

Hynes, J. (1997) *Publish and perish: Three tales of tenure and terror*, New York: Picador.

Kennedy, D. (1997) *Academic duty*, Cambridge: Harvard University Press.

Lodge, D. (1975) *Changing places: A tale of two campuses*, London: Secker & Warburg.

—— (1984) *Small world: Academic romance*, New York: Macmillan.

—— (1989) *Nice work: A novel*, New York: Viking Penguin.

Lovitts, B.E. (1996) *Leaving the ivory tower: A sociological analysis of the causes of departure from doctoral study*, Ann Arbor, MI: University of Michigan.

Malti-Douglas, F. (1998) *Hisland: Adventures in Ac-ac-ademe*, Albany, NY: SUNY Press.

National Academy of Sciences, National Academy of Engineering and Institute of Medicine (1997) *Adviser, teacher, role model, friend: On being a mentor to students in science and engineering*, Washington, DC: National Academy Press.

Pauldi, M.A. (ed.) (1996) *Sexual harassment on college campuses: Abusing the ivory power*, Albany, NY: SUNY Press.

Phelan, J. (1991) *Beyond the tenure track: 15 months in the life of an English professor*, Columbus, OH: Ohio State University Press.

Rostenberg, L. and Stern, M. (1997) *Old books, rare friends: Two literary sleuths and their shared passion*, New York: Doubleday.

Smiley, J. (1995) *Moo*, New York: Alfred A. Knopf.

Smith, P. (1990) *Killing the spirit: Higher education in America*, New York: Viking.

Sykes, C.J. (1988) *Profscam: Professors and the demise of higher education*, Washington, DC: Regenry Gateway.

Toth, E. (1997) *Ms. Mentor's impeccable advice for women in academia*, Philadelphia: University of Pennsylvania Press.

Appendix D
Suggested Reading on Research Methodology

Becker, H.S. (1986) *Writing for social scientists: How to start and finish your thesis, book, or article*, Chicago: University of Chicago Press.

Bogdan, R. and Biklen, S. (1982) *Qualitative research for educators: An introduction to theories and methods*, Boston: Allyn and Bacon.

Booth, W.C., Colomb, G.G. and Williams, J.M. (1995) *The craft of research*, Chicago: University of Chicago Press.

Brause, R.S. and Mayher, J.S. (eds.) (1991) *Search and research: What the inquiring teacher needs to know*, London: Falmer.

Briggs, C. (1986) *Learning how to ask: A sociolinguistic appraisal of the role of the interview in social science research*, New York: Cambridge University Press.

Howe, K.R. (1998) "The interpretive turn and the new debate in education," *Educational Researcher*, 27(8), 13–20.

Howe, K.R. and Eisenhart, M.A. (1990) "Standards for qualitative (and quantitative) research: A prolegomenon," *Educational Researcher*, 19(4), 2–9.

LeCompte, M.D. and Preissle, J. (1993) *Ethnography and qualitative design in educational research*, second edition, San Diego: Academic Press.

Miles, M. and Huberman, A.M. (1994) *Qualitative data analysis: A sourcebook of new methods*, second edition, Beverly Hills: Sage

Mishler, E.G. (1986) *Research interviewing: Context and narrative*, Cambridge: Harvard University Press.

Radnofsky, M.L. (1996) "Qualitative methods: Visually representing complex data in an image/text balance," *Qualitative Inquiry*, 2(4), December, 385–402.

Richardson, V. (forthcoming) *Handbook of research on teaching*, fourth edition, New York: Macmillan.

Strauss, A.L. (1987) *Qualitative analysis for social scientists*, New York: Cambridge University Press.

Wittrock, M. (ed.) (1986) *Handbook of research on teaching*, third edition, New York: Macmillan.

Appendix E
Sample Checklist of Activities

Item	Date
Provisional admission to doctoral program	
Enroll in first 12 credits	
Apply for permanent matriculation	
Prepare for permanent matriculation interview	
Appear for interview	
Receive written notification of permanent matriculation	
Complete required coursework	
Create study group for comprehensive examination	
Apply to take comprehensive examination	
Receive official notification of date, time, and place	
Take comprehensive examination	
Receive official notification of passing comprehensive examination	
Identify potential research topic	
Identify potential faculty for dissertation committee	
Request a professor to be your mentor or to chair your dissertation committee	
Get advice about potential readers from your mentor/chair	
Identify specific research question/problem	
Write Chapter 1 of your dissertation proposal	
Write Chapter 2 of your dissertation proposal	
Seek feedback and approval from your mentor and readers	
Write Chapter 3 of your dissertation proposal	
Obtain approval of your committee	
Present your proposal for review and approval	

Receive official notification of the approval of your proposal	
Obtain approvals for your data collection	
Pilot test your instruments and/or procedures	
Revise procedures as needed	
Collect data for your study	
Analyze the data you collected	
Present draft of analysis to mentor/chair	
Revise draft as discussed	
Present draft to mentor and readers	
Revise as needed	
Obtain approval from your committee to "schedule your orals"	
Schedule oral interview/examination	
Discuss expectations with chair/mentor	
Successfully complete your oral examination	
Revise as needed	
Submit your dissertation for editorial review	
Revise as requested	
Submit revised, edited dissertation	
File for graduation	
Graduate, Doctor!	

References

American Psychological Association (1994) *Publication manual of the American Psychological Association*, Washington, DC: APA.

Bolig, R.A. (1982) "The ambivalent decision," in A. Vartuli (ed.), *The Ph.D. experience*, New York: Praeger.

Booth, W.C., Colomb, G.G. and Williams, J.M. (1995) *The craft of research*, Chicago: University of Chicago Press.

Bowen, W.G. and Rudenstine, N.L. (1992) *In pursuit of the PhD*, Princeton, NJ: Princeton University Press.

Brause, R.S. (1997) "What are the effects of completing a dissertation?" Paper presented at the annual meeting of the Eastern Educational Research Association, Hilton Head Island, SC, February.

Brause, R.S. and Mayher, J.S. (eds.) (1991) *Search and re-search: What the inquiring teacher needs to know*, London: Falmer.

Brown, D. (1997) "Tales of a thesis writer," *The Harvard Crimson*, March 5, 2.

Fahrenthold, D.A. (1997) "Facing the faculty: Steven Ozment brings history home," *Harvard Crimson*, February 7, 3.

Gilles, C. (1996) "Everybody needs a 'grip:' Support groups for doctoral students," in E.F. Whitmore and Y.M. Goodman (eds.), *Whole language voices in teacher education*, York, ME: Stenhouse.

Hawley, P. (1993) *Being bright is not enough: The unwritten rules of doctoral study*, New York: Charles C. Thomas.

Haworth, K. (1999) "Push to hire Ph.D.'s as professors," *The Chronicle of Higher Education*, January 8, A12–13.

Holland, D.C. and Eisenhart, M.A. (1990) *Educated in romance: Women, achievement, and college culture*, Chicago: University of Chicago Press.

Howe, K.R. (1998) "The interpretive turn and the new debate in education," *Educational Researcher*, 27(8), 13–20.

Howe, K.R. and Eisenhart, M.A. (1990) "Standards for qualitative (and quantitative) research: A prolegomenon," *Educational Researcher*, 19(4), 2–9.

Kennedy, D. (1997) *Academic duty*, Cambridge: Harvard University Press.

Leatherman, C. (1997) "Should dog walking and house sitting be required for Ph.D.?," *The Chronicle of Higher Education*, July 18, A10–11.

LeCompte, M.D. and Goetz, J.P. (1982) "Problems of reliability and validity in ethnographic research," *Review of Educational Research*, 52(1), 31–60.

Levine, D.N. (1993) *Classroom discourse in a secondary level self-contained class for students labelled "learning disabled,"* doctoral dissertation proposal, Fordham University.

Lovitts, B.E. (1996) *Leaving the ivory tower: A sociological analysis of the causes of departure from doctoral study*, Ann Arbor, MI: University of Michigan.

Magner, D.K. (1999) "Record number of doctorates awarded in 1997," *The Chronicle of Higher Education*, January 8, A14–15.

Masters, L. (1997) "Peer interactions in the context of college peer tutoring," draft of a doctoral dissertation, Fordham University.

Menand, L. (1996) "How to make a Ph.D. matter," *The New York Times Magazine*, September 22, 78–81.

Miles, M. and Huberman, A.M. (1994) *Qualitative data analysis: A sourcebook of new methods*, second edition, Beverly Hills: Sage

Nelson, C. (1997) "Career success for some Ph.D.'s comes by leaving academe behind," *The Chronicle of Higher Education*, October 31, A12.

New York Times, The (1997) "Student wins suit accusing a professor of plagiarism," September 24, A25.

Olson, G.A. and Drew, J. (1998) "(Re)reenvisioning the dissertation in English studies," *College English*, 61(1), September, 56–66.

Richardson, V. (forthcoming) *Handbook of research on teaching*, fourth edition, New York: Macmillan.

Schneider, A. (1998) "Harvard faces the aftermath of a graduate student's suicide," *The Chronicle of Higher Education*, October 23, A12–14.

Sheehy, G. (1976) *Passages: Predictable crises of adult life*, New York: E.P. Dutton.

Sizer, T. (1997) "Lessons about school principals from the Essential Schools," presentation to Metropolitan Council of Educational Administration Programs, Fordham University.

Smith, B.D. (1982) "Taking the giant step: Writing the dissertation," in S. Vartuli (ed.), *The Ph.D. experience: A woman's point of view*, pp. 35–44, New York: Praeger.

Vartuli, S.A. (1982) A professional socialization process. Vartuli, S. (Ed.). *The Ph.D. experience: A woman's point of view*. pp. 1–14. NY: Praeger.

Wittrock, M. (Ed.) (1986) *Handbook of research on teaching*, third edition, New York: Macmillan.

Index

Page numbers in italics indicate figures and tables